MW01227050

COGNITIVE BEHAVIORAL THERAPY MADE SIMPLE

A CBT Workbook To Retrain Your Brain
For Overcoming Depression And
Anxiety By Psychotherapy

JASON COLE

© Copyright 2019 by Jason Cole
All rights reserved.

This document is geared towards providing exact and reliable information with regards to the topic and issue covered. The publication is sold with the idea that the publisher is not required to render accounting, officially permitted, or otherwise, qualified services. If advice is necessary, legal or professional, a practiced individual in the profession should be ordered.

From a Declaration of Principles which was accepted and approved equally by a Committee of the American Bar Association and a Committee of Publishers and Associations.

In no way is it legal to reproduce, duplicate, or transmit any part of this document in either electronic means or in printed format. Recording of this publication is strictly prohibited and any storage of this document is not allowed unless with written permission from the publisher. All rights reserved.

The information provided herein is stated to be truthful and consistent, in that any liability, in terms of inattention or otherwise, by any usage or abuse of any policies, processes, or directions contained within is the solitary and utter responsibility of the recipient reader. Under no circumstances will any legal responsibility or blame be held against the publisher for any reparation, damages, or monetary loss due to the information herein, either directly or indirectly.

Respective authors own all copyrights not held by the publisher.

The information herein is offered for informational purposes solely, and is universal as so. The presentation of the information is without contract or any type of guarantee assurance. The trademarks that are used are without any consent, and the publication of the trademark is without permission or backing by the trademark owner. All trademarks and brands within this book are for clarifying purposes only and are the owned by the owners themselves, not affiliated with this document

INTRODUCTION

Cognitive Therapy is a collaborative process of empirical investigation, reality testing, and problem-solving between therapist and client where the client's maladaptive interpretations and conclusions are treated as testable hypotheses. The 3 levels of cognition Beck believed influenced the cause and maintenance of pathology are Automatic thoughts, schemas, and cognitive distortions. A cognitive therapist might ask a client to keep a journal of Automatic Thoughts, which are thoughts that arise spontaneously in response to certain situations and are more a reflection of a client's appraisal of a situation rather than the actual situation itself.

Schemas (core beliefs; underlying assumptions) are internal models of the self and the world that develop over the course of experiences beginning early in life and can serve an adaptive function by allowing new information to be linked with old information, making for more efficient information processing. Beck identified systematic errors in reasoning that form the link between dysfunctional schemas and automatic thoughts, which he called Cognitive Distortions. It refers to the process of a person biasing or adapting newly processed information to fit a relevant schema. A client in therapy reports to his therapist that he is a bad employee and is likely to get fired; however, the therapist soon recognizes the client's negative conclusion cannot be supported by real evidence and, in fact, seems to go against the therapist's experience of the client as punctual, engaged, and hardworking. The cognitive distortion this client is most likely making is arbitrary inference, which occurs when specific conclusions are drawn with no evidence.

In cognitive marital therapy, a wife reports her frustration with her husband for not taking out the trash, which she says is causing a lot of problems in their marriage. Her husband, however, complains that she fails to recognize other things he does to help. Selective abstraction is the cognitive distortion most likely leading to the wife's frustration as she is focusing on a single detail that is taken out of context, at the expense of other information. The term Cognitive Restructuring refers to therapeutic techniques that attempt to alter maladaptive thought patterns that are believed to be responsible for maladaptive behavior and emotional disorders. An elderly man who was mugged by a group of teenage boys develops a hatred for all adolescents, exemplifying this cognitive distortion.

Overgeneralization Regarding cognitive distortions, a person who describes a recent trauma as "no big deal" is likely minimizing, while a person who becomes overly emotional after getting a small scratch in their car represents magnification.

Personalization is a cognitive distortion characterized by inappropriately attributing external events to oneself when no causal connection really exists (e.g., a therapist takes responsibility for her client being fired from work).

The cognitive distortion of separating experiences into 2 extremes, such as all good and all bad, is called Dichotomous Thinking. In Cognitive Therapy, negative thoughts about the self, the future, and the world are referred to as the Cognitive triad. A person who presents with cognitions of hopelessness, low self-esteem, and failure is most likely experiencing symptoms of depression, while anxiety is associated with thoughts of anticipated harm or danger.

Cognitive behavior therapy is a discipline of psychology that seeks to help people cope with dysfunctional emotions. Unlike other types of open-ended therapy, cognitive behavior therapy is goal-oriented and systematic. This type of therapy is often used for mood disorders, anxiety disorders, psychotic disorders, substance abuse, and eating disorders. In addition, the therapy has been proven effective for some of the population in treating post-traumatic stress disorder, OCD, depression and even specific disorders like bulimia nervosa.

Because of the efficacy of CBT, it is often times a very brief experience, unlike some other forms of therapy that can go on for months on end. CBT may be individually based or based inside of a group. Recently, more effort has been made to use CBT for reforming criminals in correctional settings. In these instances, therapists attempt to reeducate criminal offenders on cognitive skills and coping mechanisms that will help reduce criminal behavior.

In this process, therapists/doctors will be identifying and monitoring a patient's thoughts and beliefs. (These will be discernible through a series of tests) The goal is to determine how these beliefs are related to debilitating behavior, such as alcohol abuse, criminal behavior or so on. Cognitive behavior therapy was created in the 1960s in an effort to merge the best of behavioral therapy results with that of cognitive therapy. While these two disciplines had very different origins, they found common ground when focusing on treatment.

There are two main components to analyze in this discipline and they are also the two main theories at work: cognitive and behavioral. If you suffer from social anxiety disorder but do not want to explore the option of medication, then cognitive behavior therapy is an excellent alternative. In fact, it is currently considered the most effective form of treating social anxiety disorder, far more efficacious just medication alone.

CONTENTS

CHAPTER ONE

UNDERSTAND HOW YOUR TRAIN OF THOUGHT IS BROUGHT ABOUT

You are today where your thoughts have brought you; you will be tomorrow where your thoughts take you. **James Allen; As a Man Thinketh**

HOW THOUGHTS ARE MADE

One of the 11 Forgotten Laws, is the "Power of Thought." In my previous article, "The Law Of Attraction, I mentioned that Bob Proctor, a featured speaker in the movie, "The Secret" said that there are eleven other laws that man needs to understand if a man has the desire to have more of the abundant life that is his birthright.

Most of us have been brought up with the wrong method of using what is called the mind. Most of our lives have been crowded with all kinds of thoughts of negativity. Everywhere you turn, there are drastic news and reports. Have you checked the "News" lately? Bad news sells, for people are more interested in learning about how someone lost his/her life in a terrible accident. We are not interested in paying for good news, and we know that is true because the majority of the news coverage is of a negative nature.

There is enough sound information available on the understanding of how the mind works, at least in part, so that man can learn how to control his thoughts. This information, without doubt, should be required curriculum in every school, for every child should be raised up learning how to properly use his/her mind.

Experts tell us that most of the clutter that mankind is turning over in their mind is not "thinking," but rather a compilation of real and unreal trash that should be "deleted." (I couldn't help but use that computer word, "deleted.") (smile) Thinking is really done in the heart, remember, "As a man thinketh in his heart?" Another name for the heart is the "Subconscious Mind." This is where the thought is processed and created.

All of the content that you and I have in our lifetime received, either by reading or hearing, or experienced, has ended up in the files of the Subconscious Mind. The subconscious mind (is better than a computer), will store all of the information we've been exposed to, bad or good, and will upload what information we desire when our conscious mind requests it. I always thought I was using my conscious mind to do my thinking, but the fact is, the subconscious mind is responsible for true thought and thinking.

Think about that. If you have a question of something that you need the answer to, all you have to do is gather all of the facts pertaining to the question at hand, and submit them to your subconscious mind, and it will go to work and sift through all the data, and in due time will upload the answer to your conscious mind. It may take several days for the answered thought to show up.

When the light bulb comes on, and you jump for joy, saying, "I've got it, I've got the answer to what I've been wanting to know! Your subconscious mind diligently worked for you and provided the answer. Your conscious mind could only stand by and wait until the powerful subconscious mind did its work.

There is a great deal of detail in this process that we cannot deal with in this article for a couple of reasons, (1) a lack of time and space, and (2) because man is still learning how the Conscious and Subconscious mind work together.

You have probably heard that the conscious mind represents the portion of the iceberg that is above the water, and the subconscious mind represents the portion of the iceberg that is under the water. Needless for me to say that the subconscious mind is much greater in size and power than the conscious mind.

What is even more astounding is, where is the Subconscious Mind located? No man can tell us. Such a great mechanism, but yet not visible, and it is not the brain, OK? Wow, God is awesome! Amen?

THE LAW OF ATTRACTION - THOUGHTS

Our minds can be compared to a garden. Like a garden, our minds can be fertilized, watered and weeded or we can let them become overgrown and wild. If we plant good health seeds in our garden, water them, keep them fertilized they will grow into very useful, beautiful plants. If we neglect this garden the seeds will produce very little that will be usable.

In the same way, we would take care of a garden to produce the things we wanted and needed we must also do the same with our thoughts. If we allow constant negative thoughts, thoughts that criticize others and thoughts that are self-defeating we will not live to our potential. If instead, we cultivate thoughts that are uplifting, always find the positive in others and keep a forward thinking positive attitude, we will create an abundance of what we are seeking in our life's.

We are the master of our mind (the gardener) and must constantly be watching for negative, unproductive thoughts. You probably know that thoughts become reality, everything comes first from thought. The enlightened yogis say that the material world is nothing more than the thought that has become dense. With this in mind, I hope you see how important it is to cultivate positive, uplifting thoughts. Nothing less then your happiness, success, and dreams depend on it.

Your thoughts will determine the person you become. Every person is exactly where he should be by the law of attraction based on his thoughts. The person's thoughts have brought him to where he now stands in life. This is not by chance that a person is where he is, it is entirely brought about by the law of attraction from personal thoughts. The law of attraction does not make mistakes in the same way gravity does not make mistakes, it works in perfect balance.

We are constantly being presented with circumstances that seem like they are outside our doing. We need to realize that we are the gardeners and we are the ones who created the thoughts that brought about these circumstances. Remember the law of attraction works perfectly and will at some point bring about the situation you now face.

The question that always comes up is how to stop these negative self-defeating thoughts. There are several ways to do this, but one of the easiest ways is to replace them with a positive uplifting thought. First, you must train yourself to watch and recognize negative thoughts. When you see a negative, unwanted thought coming, interrupt it by saying to yourself something like "I am a positive, strong, forward-thinking person". The saying can be anything you like that fits with your personal taste. The important things are to keep the thought saying positive and uplifting. With a little practice, this will become second nature to you and you will see the life you live and the circumstances presented to you changing.

THE SILENT POWER OF THOUGHT

The most powerful forces in the universe are the silent forces; and in accordance with the intensity of its power does a force become beneficent when rightly directed, and destructive when wrongly employed. This is common knowledge in regard to the mechanical forces, such as steam, electricity, etc., but few have yet learned to apply this knowledge to the realm of mind, where the thought-forces (most powerful of all) are continually being generated and sent forth as currents of salvation or destruction.

Whatever your position in life may be, before you can

hope to enter into any measure of success, usefulness, and power, you must learn how to focus your thought-forces by cultivating calmness and repose. It may be that you are a businessman, and you are suddenly confronted with some overwhelming difficulty or probable disaster. You grow fearful and anxious and are at your wit's end. To persist in such a state of mind would be fatal, for when anxiety steps in, correct judgment passes out.

Now if you will take advantage of a quiet hour or two in the early morning or at night, and go away to some solitary spot, or to a room in your house where you know you will be absolutely free from intrusion, and, seat yourself in an easy attitude, you forcibly direct your mind right away from the object of anxiety by dwelling upon something in your life that is pleasing and bliss-giving, a calm, reposeful strength will gradually steal into your mind, and your anxiety will pass away.

Upon the instant that you find your mind reverting to the lower plane of worry bring it back again, and re-establish it on the plane of peace and strength. When this is fully accomplished, you may then concentrate your whole mind on the solution of your difficulty, and what was intricate and insurmountable to you in your hour of anxiety will be made plain and easy, and you will see, with that clear vision and perfect judgment which belong only to a calm and untroubled mind, the right course to pursue and the proper end to be brought about.

You might have to try this day after day before you will be able to perfectly calm your mind, but if you persevere you will certainly accomplish it. And the course which is presented to you in that hour of calmness must be carried out. Doubtless, when you are again involved in the business of the day, and worries again creep in and begin to dominate you, you will begin to think that the course is wrong or foolish one, but do not entertain such suggestions. Be guided absolutely and entirely by the vision of calmness, and not by the shadows of anxiety. The hour of calmness is the hour of illumination and correct judgment. By such a course of mental discipline, the scattered thought-forces are reunited, and directed, like the rays of the search-light, upon the problem at issue, with the result that it gives way before them.

Have you recognized the power of your thoughts? For that matter, have you recognized just how powerful thoughts are? Take a quick inventory of everything around you. You will notice that everything (the computer, walls, light fixtures, writing tools, etc, etc) was once a thought in someone's mind. Someone dreamed of everything that we use and take for granted.

Realize that we all have the power of thought. If we think negatively about something then negative results will manifest in physical forms. If we think positively, we will produce positive manifestations. Your mind has the power to determine what your physical reality will be. If you don't, believe me, that's fine but look around you.

You may not be able to change the circumstances in which you were brought in to, but you can determine where you are going. Your thoughts along with the desire will power and determination will bring those thoughts into realities. You have total control over how you think. You are only limited by your imagination. If you allow others to influence how you think then, that is your decision just understand that in the end, you are allowing to decide how you live your life.

All successful people have thought and dreamed of their success. They have visualized what it is that they will be doing and proceed to take action. They believe in themselves and thus are not limited to what they may not have or know. The consistent theme is that it begins in their mind. It begins with a thought.

YOU ARE NOT YOUR THOUGHTS

There is a real YOU-the infinite consciousness that you are that is not your body, your mind, or your emotions, as strange as that may seem. The "you" having the life experience provides information to your brain based on external stimuli because YOU are here in a body having experiences that use the fives senses to do so. But you are always, always more than that. When you have that feeling that says, "I know I'm more than this," you're right!

Life feels difficult and perplexing at times, or a good deal of the time, because you've believed the five-sense "you" is the real one, as well as everything the five senses input into your brain, which your brain then decodes to make some sense of that information so you can interpret "reality". The sense we make of the information is more often than not colored by our beliefs and our conditioning because the brain filters signals we receive about "reality" to fit our beliefs. Sir Francis Bacon said: "The world is not to be narrowed till it will go into the understanding... but the understanding to be expanded and opened till it can take in the image of the world as it is in fact."

You want to look at what you believe and who you believe it for. If it isn't for YOU, you want to look at that as well. You see, restrictive beliefs result in a restrictive experience of "reality", rather than a big-picture, holistic one. Restrictive beliefs, especially rigid ones, suppress our ability to open and expand consciousness. As we expand our consciousness (actually, lift the veil hiding our consciousness from us), we expand how our brain decodes information it receives; we discern differently because we have more information and an improved means to process it. We and how we experience life expands. That's the only direction we and life can go in once we remind ourselves to expand our consciousness. You can have something of an experience of who the real YOU is if you watch Jill Bolte Taylor's TED.com video about her Stroke of Insight, where she had a direct experience of full consciousness as one with All There Is compared to the I-am-Jill's mind and separate, when she had a stroke that closed off her ability to interpret, in the standard manner, the signals her brain received about the world around her.

The five-sense "you" relies on those senses to navigate the life experience. YOU use the five senses but you have a sixth sense (maybe more) called intuition, or inner knowing. Intuition (inner knowing) is not an anomaly just for some. We all have it. I learned this as a fact when I went through the Silva Mind Method training a few decades ago. Even the strongest disbelievers in the class performed, as we had to, to graduate.

Intuition, or inner knowing, is one way we plug into the infinite consciousness we are and are a part of. The esoteric ones of old and a number of our contemporaries knew and know this. We may not be brought up to know this about ourselves, we may even be told it's a "sin" to use this part of our true nature, but it's still there for us, ready to assist our navigation through life in ways we desire but don't necessarily feel skilled at using. But we can put it into practice.

Your five senses can cause you to believe the "matrix" is real, that what the senses perceive is all there is, which is quite different from the real All There Is-the One Source, which is limitless in what it can supply and provide for you, and does. The interesting thing about this is that quantum mechanics has proven that nothing, nothing, is there. The only thing there or here is the consciousness creating the appearance of reality, which is a pretty impressive hologram, so impressive that we can literally bump our heads on it. Ernest Homes wrote, "Nothing moves but the mind." He wrote this quite a while before quantum mechanics caught up with this as a fact.

This is an extraordinarily challenging truth for most of us to believe, much less grasp, because though true, it's contrary to what most believe because of what we were taught and are still being taught, despite the empirical evidence (and ancient knowing). Humans managed to accept that Earth wasn't the center of the universe and was round, not flat (once they knew they wouldn't be punished or worse for believing that, and once those in authority could no longer get away with insisting it was flat, etc.). But this fact about the reality we're looking at here is a bit harder to wrap the mind around because we've believed the opposite for so long and because of how effective the physics of it all is, as well as what we're told "reality" is.

When thoughts happen, someone in your case YOU- is there to notice them. When a person's body stops, their infinite consciousness departs the body suit but doesn't cease to exist. This is evidenced by out-of-body experiences, near-death experiences, and more. Even though we know of these experiences or know people who've had them, or have had them ourselves, we still don't necessarily integrate the full meaning for us into our daily lives.

Many of us who've been on the spiritual or metaphysical path say we believe we're infinite consciousness. Do we really believe it, or understand it? If we're infinite consciousness after we leave the body, then we're infinite consciousness right now. When we believe only what our five senses supply us with that our brains decode and we (our "you" aspects) then interpret based on how we were conditioned by the various systems in place that holds so much influence over us and our lives (which influences past, present, and future perceptions and experiences), we cut ourselves off from our full, true nature. We say we want to be authentic, but what does that mean to us? Will we include the fact we are more than our thoughts and emotions and body? Or that, in fact, we are not them, that we simply use them while we're here?

We don't like feeling limited, but we aren't too excited about going the distance with what's being discussed here. In fact, it can be frightening because we'll have to step away from the tribal mentality, which might make the tribe leaders and members a bit peeved with us. (Ever wondered why that is?) Just that thought, or acting on it, can make us feel alone, but only until we find others who understand and live this. Not going the distance is making a choice, one we're not happy with the results of but are used to, or conditioned to be used to, or are afraid to accept and allow.

We identify with our thoughts, and when we do so, we believe they express absolute truth. All you have to do is have one of your assumptions proven false to see this, which is a minimal form or example of this. We have tens of thousands of thoughts each day. We, as our five-sense "you", may believe we need to believe each of those thoughts, simply because they're there. You may recall the revelation that subliminal messages are placed in movies and commercials and more to influence people to buy products or believe whatever. Are those your thoughts? Did you choose them? You can choose your thoughts, just as you can choose which item on the stock exchange ticker tape to pay attention to or focus on. You really can.

Is it easy to remember you're more than your thoughts, more than what the five senses indicate you are? Not necessarily, because every day you wake up and set about dealing with whatever you deal with. What's going on around you or "you", based on your beliefs, can convince you to be busy in action or have busy-mind, rather than the productive-constructive mind, or relaxed mind, which is usually when inner knowing communicates with us. With either or both of these busy aspects going on, who feels they have time or energy to remember he or she is infinite consciousness having a human experience? But we can remember this, even amid the busyness of our lives.

It is important to make time or remember to plug into the Truth of who we are and into our connection with the One Source so we don't get lost in illusions and delusions. Otherwise, we're prone to believe we're weak rather than strong, stuck rather than creative and innovative, limited rather than infinite, not in control of our choices when we can be, and so on even though some days or during some experiences, we feel limited more than infinite; but we can remember and recover our footing, if we know about this in the first place.

It will also help to know and remember that two of the parts of your brain are the R-complex, which is responsible for our fight, flight, or freeze reactions, and the neocortex, which helps us think things through. In the briefest of nutshells, you have both the ability to react based on whether you feel safe or not, which is based on your thoughts about events, as well as the ability to think about your thoughts a bit before you react. One reason we feel we can't think straight or with more conscious consideration when we're having strong (negative) emotions is that the R-complex is activated to ensure survival. This is why we can think straight, or more consciously, when we're relaxed, without busy-mind.

The R-complex cannot distinguish between the past and present and is why your body responds to a negative memory as though "it's" happening now, which causes you to behave as though your survival is at stake, even if you're lying in a hammock, with everything quiet all around you. If you rely on the R-complex too often or too much, you don't exercise the neocortex. You then create brain "ruts" that lead you down the path of reactive behavior more than create neuronal "paths" that lead to conscious consideration. This alone may inspire you to become aware of thoughts and aware of the thinker.

How can you distinguish between thoughts and inner knowing? Thoughts have a loudness quality to them: they're insistent. Inner knowing is subtle. It will nudge you once or twice then go quiet if you don't listen. You can practically feel thoughts in your head, almost like a movie screen on your forehead facing inward. You feel inner knowing in your chest center, maybe you even feel it radiate into your limbs, but you don't feel it in your head. Put another way, you feel it in your heart-energy center, not in your mind.

Your thoughts may lead you to want to be considered clever (after all, cleverness is rewarded), which your mind, through thoughts, can accommodate; but clever and wise are not the same thing. Wisdom is something your infinite consciousness provides. Cleverness without wisdom can be disastrous. It can lead to creating things or taking actions that do more short- and long-term harm than any real good, because cleverness doesn't always consider ethics, morality, justice, and overall well-being, whereas infinite consciousness always does. Cleverness AND wisdom is a beneficial combination. We can look at our own lives and at what's going on around us to see when cleverness, wisdom, or the combination is used, and when they are not.

Our thoughts based on only five senses keep us occupied, so occupied that we often can't see the bigger picture going on around us. However, we can choose to put our attention on our connection to the One Source so we keep in mind who we really are, which is not the thoughts we have and not the thoughts we're told to have or are influenced to have by anyone else. We can look at what's going on in us and around us and ascertain whether we follow the path the One Source would encourage or the herd. When we realize we're not our thoughts, we can think and feel and know for ourselves, and do so from a higher perspective, a perspective more akin to the One Source than the "matrix". It's a good practice, one you'll appreciate.

THOUGHTS AND FEELINGS AND EMOTIONAL INTELLIGENCE

1. You cannot control every thought you have but you can control the flow of your thoughts.

The most important thing to understand is the difference between initial and reactive or response or thoughts. An initial thought is one that either just pops into your mind for no apparent reason.

It is impossible to control every initial thought, although as we will see, managing your state can influence the frequency of unwarranted initial thoughts. Reactive or response of thoughts can and should be controlled and managed in an effective and constructive way, it's called emotional intelligence.

2. Feelings usually trail behind thoughts.

A series of thoughts usually leads to a certain state of feeling. At times as happens quite quickly wanted others the delay may be longer. This is important to understand if one is to gain mastery over oneself.

3. The direction of the flow of your thoughts will

usually determine the direction of your feelings.

Most of the time a single thought does not determine the state of your feelings. Your state is usually the result of a sequence of thoughts. If that sequence is negative, your feelings will deteriorate. But if the sequence of thought is positive, your feelings will improve.

If you can't control an initial thought but you can control the reactive and responsive thoughts, then managing our state of feeling rests on us managing the direction of the flow of our thoughts

4. Feelings put power behind your thoughts when your thoughts and feelings are synchronized.

Thoughts and feelings work together to create upward and downward spirals; a few happy thoughts and you start to feel better, feeling better empowers you to think more happy thoughts which in turn make you feel even better. That's a positive upward spiral. But it works just as effectively the other way around; a few unhappy thoughts and you start feeling worse, feeling worse make you think more unhappy thoughts which in turn make you feel even worse. That's a negative downward spiral.

5. The rate of change in both upward and downward spirals will accelerate the longer and

more intensely they are synchronized.

Unless checked in some way, upward and downward spirals will continue to cycle faster and faster. When a positive cycle accelerates it can lead to euphoria which, although enjoyable, can lead to certain negative results such as poor decision-making and burnout. Thankfully our own natural cycles and common sense usually moderate tendency.

However, for most of us, it is the unchecked downward spiral that usually causes the most problems as downward spirals are most destructive of our own well-being and relationships. Learning how to manage negative cycles is an important part of emotional intelligence.

6. Feelings disempower thoughts when they are not synchronized.

If your thoughts and feelings are flowing in one direction, changing the direction of your thoughts is a lot more difficult than when your feelings are synchronized with the direction you want your thoughts to go. Your state of feeling disempowers your initial training of thought; in other words, you have to work harder to change direction then you do keep going in the same direction. That works in most things in life.

7. There are more thoughts than feelings.

To demonstrate the point let us say that there are 10 thoughts for every feeling. This is good news because by monitoring a few feelings were able to keep tabs on many thoughts. Whatever we are feeling at a particular moment is, for example, the result of the past 10 thoughts.

So, in a very simple sense, we can look back and see what direction our thoughts are moving in. That one feeling has alerted us to train of thought that is leading in a particular direction.

8. There are natural cycles and rhythms in life.

These natural cycles and rhythms do influence our ability to control our thoughts and feelings; it is important to understand that they influence but do not control our ability. There are also unnatural states that are caused by such things as chemical imbalances and injuries, these also have an impact on our ability to control thoughts and feelings.

Understanding and compassion, for both ourselves and others, is important; things are not always what they seem.

Our goal, therefore, is to manage the thoughts (and resultant feelings) that we can and should control, as well as moderating the effects of natural and unnatural cycles and rhythms.

9. The key to self-mastery is self-awareness.

Self-awareness is the key to self-mastery, to managing our thoughts by monitoring our feelings. Our feelings are a feedback system, they tell us how well we are managing our thoughts.

Understanding what you want to feel is the starting point. Decide what state you want to live in and then monitor your feelings in relation to that state. If you want to be happy self-awareness will alert you to any state that isn't in harmony with happiness. Having been alerted to do this unwanted state you'll be able to check back through your past thoughts and identify where this unwanted state arose.

This could take a fraction of a second or may need some careful contemplation but either way, self-awareness gives you the opportunity to create and manage the state you want.

10. Have fun, be happy.

This is the core of emotional intelligence.

WHY YOU ARE ADDICTED TO YOUR THOUGHTS

Regurgitated Thoughts

Who would you be without your thoughts?

Who is the person you call "I" reading these words right now?

Ponder these questions while I give you an insight into something I experienced whilst meditating some years ago. One evening, towards the end of a meditation session I experienced a brief episode of no thoughts. It scared me, though I recognize my thoughts once more in the next instance. It was as though I had gone off-line for a short period of time. What frightened me most about the experience was the notion I didn't exist. If there is no experience of thoughts, who am I? My thoughts confirm my existence and so I felt at ease when I began to experience them once more.

We are addicted to thoughts without realizing it. I mean that in the kindest way. Our experience of thoughts confirms our presence within the fabric of reality. It was the French philosopher René Descartes who once proclaimed: "I think, therefore I am." This is a persuasive declaration that suggests our thoughts give rise to our humanity and experience of reality. In a similar vein, psychologist and author Loch Kelly confirms our compulsive addiction to thoughts when he writes in Shift into Freedom: The Science and Practice of Open-Hearted Awareness: "The habit of continually looking to thoughts for satisfaction, even positive thoughts, creates a similar kind of addiction."

From the moment we're born until our passing, we process anywhere between 60,000 to 80,000 thoughts a day. Many of those are regurgitated from the previous day; rarely do we think anything new. For example, when was the last time you had an original thought or were moved by a powerful insight? Was it days, weeks or months? We are accustomed to thinking the same thoughts day in day out and wonder why we live monotonous lives. It was the founder of Hay House, the late Louise Hay who once wrote: "You are not a helpless victim of your own thoughts, but rather a master of your mind."

If we were to observe our thoughts more often, we would notice they are habitual and dictated by past conditioning, our level of awareness and perception of the world. This explains why we are addicted to thoughts because we trust them to be true. I'm not suggesting this is bad, however, our addiction to thinking can lead us astray and cause stress if we don't make time to disconnect from our thoughts.

Loch Kelly says we can change our addiction to

automatic thoughts by observing them instead of becoming invested in them: "Paying attention to automatic thoughts is simply a habit we can change. When you shift into awareness-based knowing, automatic thinking moves into the background, and you experience true peace of mind."

Break The Addiction To Thoughts

Our thoughts are our best friend and our worst enemy. They come and go from our mind and even though they are impermanent, it often feels like they have taken up residence in our mind like squatters refusing to leave. No matter how hard you try to remove negative thoughts, they keep showing up. What if it isn't necessary to drive them away, but see them as the sum of the thinking process?

What I mean is, negative thoughts is a label we assign to disempowering thoughts we don't like. I would argue that they can be useful and our task is to integrate them into the wholeness of our being instead of trying to banish them. Thoughts are addictive when we cannot be alone in silence for more than five minutes. This is the feedback I've received over many years from clients who are stressed. When I invite them to find five minutes a day to meditate, they'd rather have a surgical procedure performed than be alone with their thoughts.

Many people flee from the voices in their head by being preoccupied with activities that distract them from being alone. This is apparent whether through socializing, gossiping, checking social media, consuming alcohol or addictive foods. These are distractions that prevent us from coming home to the quiet stillness of our core self. It needn't be that way. It is possible to reclaim your thoughts and not be consumed by them. However, it takes practice and diligence to see past the narrative they promote while recognizing you are not your thoughts but one who experiences them.

Thoughts will always have a narrative to persuade us of something that is wrong in the world. We are naturally drawn to this and create a dialogue which later forms our character. These events start when we follow the trail of thoughts down a slippery slope.

To break our addiction to thoughts, we must first realize their impermanent nature. This helps us to discern the transient nature of thoughts and that we needn't bind ourselves to them. Rather, we see them as a mental occurrence that comes and goes like ocean waves crashing into the shoreline. When we let go of our addiction to thoughts, we realize a powerful undercurrent beneath them, in the form of expansive love and that my dear friends is who we really are.

A GUIDE TO RECLAIMING YOUR THOUGHTS

Persistent Thoughts

Your thoughts have the power to shape your life.

Many people believe their thoughts are set in stone and cannot be changed. Maybe this is due to naivety mostly. Since you cannot see a thought, it's considered something that happens to you rather than through you.

I started journaling long ago as a result of my frustrations and to observe my thinking. My thoughts seemed scattered at the time, as though unraveling a cotton ball. To make sense of it was futile.

However, upon waking up the next morning, thoughts were tranquil and peaceful. They bore a resemblance to the ocean tides, sometimes furious yet other times calm and composed. Nevertheless, it was difficult to see a pattern.

How could thoughts be out of control one day and peaceful the next? I was unaware of what contributed to the change.

You may be wondering how to tame your thoughts given their uncertainty.

The universal perspective states if you stop resisting the flow of thoughts, no matter how oppressive, they will rescind into the background of your mind. Yet the more attention and energy you award them, the more they grow in intensity. This is known as being a silent witness to your thoughts, like waves crashing into the shoreline.

It must be said you are not your thoughts and thinking does not constitute who you are. Thoughts come and go, so there's no point in attaching yourself to individual thoughts.

To cultivate empowering thoughts is challenging since we are under the influence of our external environment. Those who entertain positive thoughts realize life flows in a peaceful manner, as opposed to those under the influence of negative thoughts.

The benefits of nurturing positive thoughts include:

1. Reduction in stress levels: Your thoughts will oscillate in a steady flow, with no peaks and troughs. Stress is caused by external stimuli which produce internal unrest.

2. Improved sense of wellbeing and health: You're less likely to entertain thoughts of lack, ill-health, disease and pain since you recognize the mechanism underlying destructive thinking.

3. Better coping mechanisms: Your threshold or tolerance levels improve. What set you off before now has little impact on you. You are stable and less likely to react to external stressors.

4. More successful: Those who nurture positive thoughts navigate their way through life's dramas. They're less affected by their external world. This is clear when playing the stock market. It was Warren Buffet who quipped, "Until you can manage your emotions, you'll never master money."

5. Problems give way to opportunities: Those who harness the natural flow of thoughts are orientated towards opportunities instead of problems. Their minds are geared toward success and prosperity instead of lack. The ability to navigate your way out of harmful situations through the power of positive thinking is empowering.

HOW TO RECLAIM YOUR POWER

How do you know your thoughts are in harmony?

Look no further than your inner world. What upset you earlier, will have little effect now. I've noted my reaction to other people's emotional insecurities is less nowadays. I stay composed, knowing it takes a lot to destabilize me because I am in control of my mental wellbeing.

However, in my early adult life, I was insecure and inadequate, with impaired self-esteem. My mind processed unwanted thoughts and it led me nowhere fast, except recalling useless internal dialogues which achieved little.

However, meditation helped.

To be in silence with my thoughts allowed me to transform my daily living habits. If you're unaccustomed to meditation, I urge you to consider incorporating it into your life. You needn't start the way Eastern tradition espouses. Integrate it slowly into your life by finding time in your daily schedule. Start with as little as five minutes a day and work up to twenty minutes or more, as your body becomes accustomed to it.

People cringe at the notion of spending time alone in silence. They need noise and others around them to validate their existence.

Your soul is the quiet voice which speaks in whispers. To retreat into silence provides a perfect space for that voice to be heard. If you struggle to sit in silence for ten minutes or more, I suggest easing your way into the practice until it becomes an adopted habit.

It requires time and patience to adjust to new behavior, particularly when nurturing positive thoughts. Avoid pushing too hard when starting out, take your time to enjoy the experience and learn to be comfortable with silence.

When you perceive your thoughts are out of balance, pause for a moment and take a deep breath. Don't try to silence them, as doing so means resisting what is. Your natural state is peace and harmony. Make an inner declaration to awaken this calmness, instead of being a victim to the endless mental chatter.

To navigate thoughts is akin to driving a car. You might speed up, brake, corner and slow down depending on the road conditions ahead. Your thoughts have the same influence. You become a passenger without a steering wheel, following the trail of thoughts until they dissolve into the background of your mind.

When your thoughts are out of control, instead of resisting them, follow their lead. Since you're not attached to the outcome, take note of the main themes of the thoughts. As a result, you build awareness and direct your attention toward calmer waters. "Where Attention goes Energy flows; Where Intention goes Energy flows," states author James Redfield.

You CANNOT stop unwanted thoughts because

what you resist persists. Your resistance to what it becomes the source of suffering, which fuels more of the same suffering.

To break the cycle, go with the FLOW of thoughts. Most of all, don't take yourself seriously. You will learn and grow, which means stepping out of your comfort zone and occasionally making mistakes.

Personal growth means roadblocks will arise to test you from time to time. Your mission, if you accept, is to allow the experience to unfold while discovering the valuable lessons that lie within each experience.

HOW THOUGHTS AND THE WAY YOU FEEL TRIGGERS ANXIETY

Have you ever felt as if your thoughts are controlling your every decision? That you want to do something but there is simply no motivation? If so, maybe you have wondered how to cope with panic attacks or prevent the terrible feelings brought on by anxiety.

When we are faced with an adverse situation, we are more likely to favor a negative outcome rather than positive. Why is this? The truth of the matter is that the whole lives we have been trained to automatically integrate and obsess over the thoughts we bring forth. So essentially when we are faced with an unfamiliar project or uncomfortable situation, it is natural to feel scared or anxious because it is usually doubt or fear that takes control.

The feelings that we get when anxiety is present are due to a lack or failure to see a clear outcome. This is very important in understanding how to cope with panic attacks and anxiety. Have you ever noticed when you are absolutely certain something will happen or can see a clear outcome that you are usually quick to take action or have good feelings towards it? We do this naturally without hesitation because in our minds we have established a clear path in which we can get to where we want to go; thus there is no room for anxiety or contradictory thoughts.

It is no different from feeding a pet or achieving a goal. The only difference is being absolutely clear and having a plan to achieve what it is you desire or need to be done. When we fail to see a clear outcome the next best thing that our mind can do is panic and worry, which is where anxiety tends to get the best of us. Clarity and a clear plan on how to fix what is bothering you are essential when it comes to understanding how to deal with panic attacks properly.

When you complete a task or something that has been put off for a while, whether it is a workout or project, it may sometimes feel as if you have achieved nothing. Much like the effect homework has on students. That is why homework can be such a hassle and not such an enjoyable experience. This is due to the feelings the student may have towards completing the homework. When all a student does is procrastinate and dread the next day's homework, it creates temporary comfort once the assignment is actually completed. And it is the same story the next day or assignment. This is ineffective because success without fulfillment is ultimately failure.

It can sometimes feel as if there is rarely a comfortable plan of action or pleasant potential outcome in which it would be worth taking action. Instead of temporary comfort, you must begin to see more potential in every day things and start considering other outcomes rather than the worst. Allow the creation process. Think about how good it is going to feel to get the homework done or how easy it is going to be rather than how badly you don't want to do it. You can apply this same approach to all aspects of your life. This is how to cope with panic attacks in a natural and self-satisfying way.

HOW YOUR MIND AND BELIEFS INFLUENCE YOUR BODY

There is scientific evidence to support the common theory that our 'mindset' governs our lives.

So, whether we have a thought, belief, or a gut feeling - each one will create an electrical impulse which results in emotion and the emotion then instigate a reaction. Most of our life is a series of reactions, meaning that we are basically only responding to data input - this also includes responses from our five senses - sight, smell, taste, touch, and hearing.

The emotions we feel from each experience will depend on our history, how things got recorded, how we saw the initial experience and who and what had any external control over that first experience. After a period of time, any recording is stored deep within our unconscious and each time we experience an event thereafter, our fully automated re-action system within our unconscious is brought into play over and over again.

Our unconscious cannot think for itself - it only follows instructions based on repetitive thought. Meaning, if you think the same thing over and over again, no matter what it is, your unconscious will adopt it as a belief and you are stuck with it.

Although we think we are responding directly to current thought, the response to our thought already pre-exists. By the time we are adults, only 5% of our thinking governs our actions; it is in our unconscious where the other 95% is, that really rules our lives. This is what creates our emotional responses, feelings, and repetitive patterns of behavior and this is where it has to be changed in order to bring about a different response in us.

So if you are wondering why things aren't changing as fast as you would like - it is because, your unconscious has to re-write the manual and that takes time, patience and repetitive over-writing, through consciously changing your thoughts and creating a new Mindset for yourself.

The good news is there are tools to help, e.g. Tapping, Emotional Freedom Technique, Statements, Positive Thought, NLP, Hypnotherapy and much, much, more. Finding out about the Body and the way it works chemically and electrically can help too.

Any information that gives you a greater understanding will shift you in the right direction. If you have an illness, depression, whatever it is, learning to understand ourselves and how we work is invaluable. It empowers us to take control and releases us from a feeling of helplessness.

HOW TO CHANGE YOUR THOUGHTS AND CHANGE YOUR LIFE

Parenting Your Brain

How to stop doing what you're doing if it's doing no good!

We have all done things that we know are not in our best interest. "I just couldn't help myself," is worn plea therapists and coaches frequently hear from new clients. They come with stories of regret, stories or frustration, stories of stories gone badly, and stories of behavior that brought them pain. Broken relationships lost jobs, panic attacks, slide back into the addiction - and so these circles of life seem to eternally repeating for those who have not learned the skills necessary to be the master of their choices.

For those people, the decision to finally sit face-to-face with a therapist or coach is a brave last and desperate attempt to make changes, to choose better decisions, and experience a happier successful life. And finally, in a pro-active therapeutic relationship, they are given the chance to learn a fundamental key to success.

Clients in a pro-active therapeutic or coaching relationship learn how to care for and parent the one organ in their body that is amazingly complex and equally simple - their brain. Every organ in your body has a job, your heart pumps blood, your stomach digests food, and your brain's job is to create thoughts to protect you.

The thoughts your brain creates to protect you are based on the information that has been input since your birth. Much like a software program that has been built on a set of rules and fixed strings of code, so too your brain will run its programs based on the information it has accumulated throughout your history. Would you expect a computer program built in the 70s or 80s to effectively run on your computer today? For best results, you would install updates or the latest version. So too we must update and re-program the software in our brain to give us satisfactory results in today's world.

Relatively recent research in the area of neuroplasticity has shown us we can re-program our brains. Like most skills, it can be learned, and a talented therapist can teach you these skills. Neuroplasticity is a fascinating area of research. There are plenty of articles online and on our website if you wish to learn more.

An excellent first start is imagining and clearly articulating the kind of choices you wish to be able to make on a regular basis. Not unlike building an avatar online, sit down and write out all the characteristics and types of behavior you would like to be part of the new you. Give some serious thought to the kind of person you would like others to see you as such as strong, compassionate, thoughtful, bold, happy, adventurous, a great parent, a loyal friend, a dependable partner or more. List out these characteristics and create on paper a profile of this avatar, and soon to be new you.

At the same time start considering your brain as a well-meaning, but stubborn child, who may not always know best. It is trying to protect you, based on its old programming, so be thankful. Don't beat yourself up anymore then you would beat a child for unknowingly misbehaving. If you want to effect change, it is easier of the two of you are getting along! Change is not a battle, but a journey. Too often our brain views change as a threat and will kick up every thought imaginable to stop you from change, no matter how helpful your wisest self know the change to be.

At your most primal levels, your brain still processes information and learning based on a fight or flight response. By refusing to go to battle with your primal self, and accepting and understanding these primal responses in the same way a parent accepts and understands the challenges of a petulant child, you can lessen the voices of fear that fight change. Be a good parent to your brain, loving, understanding, and firm in what you know to be right.

Armed with this knowledge seek out a therapist who understands neuroplasticity and who you consider a wise and compassionate teacher. Good Therapy is a journey of learning to be a better and happier person.

Learning how to lovingly parent your brain is a fundamental skill you need to create the life of your choosing

CHAPTER TWO

LINK BETWEEN SPIRITUALITY AND SELF-HELP

SELF-HELP GROUP

If you are serious about spiritual growth and self-help, then a group is practically indispensable in getting you where you need to go. It is a fundamental truth in psychology and self-help that you simply cannot overcome your problems alone. You need people who have been where you are and who have gone through the struggles you likely will go through as well. Even if your problem is the inability to be alone, it is likely that you can get some help from other people who use to be afraid of this but who found a way to face their fear and are now completely comfortable with being alone.

A self-help group is one of the best ways to make a serious change because the others in the group will keep you honest. We all know how to lie to ourselves and pretend as though we are making a change even when we are not. We run from place to place talking about how we want to change and reading every book in sight but we are experts at avoiding the true issue beneath the surface. Our biggest fears are buried deep inside and we look for any way to avoid them so that we would not have to face ourselves. Self-help groups force us to be honest because everyone there can see through our lies and it becomes much harder to continue the same old behavior that we have been doing up until now.

As an example, it will help to consider some specific problems that people struggle with and eventually find help in a self-help group. One of the most common of these is alcoholism. For years, alcoholics rationalize their problem with drinking and go through scores of relationships wherein they will do and say anything in order to continue drinking. Divorce, loss of a job, loss of house and loss of family are all typical patterns for alcoholics even if these losses take place over the course of decades. Eventually, the alcoholic looks back over their life and realizes they have been running from one simple truth. They can not stop drinking. Hundreds of people had already seen the problem in the alcoholic but they could not see it themselves. The last place on Earth they wanted to go was a self-help group. Desperation and disaster finally leave them no other option and they fall into AA to ask for help.

Another common example that we see over and over in self-help groups is the pattern of controlling behavior. People tend to avoid the fact that they are powerless over others and seek out relationships where they can control someone either through money or manipulation, always feeling that they are never satisfied with anyone they meet. They struggle with anger issues and feelings of rage when they do not get what they want and their marriages and relationships with their children suffer as a result. Finding themselves at the end of their rope, they may finally turn to a counselor or therapist for help but find that no therapist seems "good enough" for them either. Because of a problem that is simply too big to ignore, they may stay around the therapist's office for several months and, if they are lucky enough to listen to an expert just a little, they may finally have a breakthrough where they can finally see their own self-centered behavior up close. Therapists are trained to help a person see their own behavior in a way that is impossible for them to see on their own. It is a big difference between a person who can say they are a "control freak" and a person who can actually employ the courage to experience the fear of letting go. This is what others can help us to do and why self-help groups are now so successful.

As much as we all wish we could do it all on our own, nobody is all-powerful and we all can benefit from an outside perspective once in a while. As the famous saying goes, "You can not unscrew your screwed up head with your screwed up head!" Having the humility to see that you need a little help might just bring you the courage to seek one out. Your spiritual growth will be increased tenfold when you follow through and make a self-help group part of your ongoing spiritual progress.

AWAKENING THE SPIRITUAL SELF WITH TAROT

Awaken our spiritual self with Tarot? What does Tarot have to do with spirituality?

Well, a lot... if you let it.

There is a dimension of the spirit; a dimension where we are tapped into the consciousness of the Universe. This spiritual dimension resides within our own mind. When we tap into and awaken this consciousness we develop our intuition.

Intuition is simply being attuned to the Universal Consciousness. A Tarot is a tool for developing our intuition. It is a metaphor for the path of self-discovery and for the archetypal journey of the hero.

Anthony Louis says in Tarot Plain and Simple, "It is a device for meditation, reflection, contemplation, problem analysis, brainstorming, decision clarification, stimulation of intuition, self-understanding, spiritual growth and divination."

Through the Tarot, we look into the deepest parts of ourselves to find the answers that were there all the time. They are not necessarily predictive but often turn out to be so. It is a way of going within that spiritual dimension to find out the truth of the path we are on at that time.

When we use the Tarot, we begin to open the psychic centers of our mind; our psychic self. Our psychic self is our spiritual self. When we do anything to awaken our spiritual self, we begin the path to our spiritual awakening.

Most of the great stories in our world are about the journey of the hero. It was a very common theme for the great novels and epic poems of the past. The hero is one who has a task set before him to save all that he loves from certain danger. He must leave the comfort and safety of his home and travel to unfamiliar places and meet unfamiliar people along the way.

He will learn much about himself as he journeys and will become stronger and wiser for the journey. Along the way, he must confront and conquer his own fear in the face of evil and certain death. After his triumph, he will be able to return to his home the victor and conquering hero knowing that he has been able to save all that he holds dear-and with a new and better understanding of who he is.

Even our modern great stories are about the journey of the hero. Star Wars and Harry Potter are just two examples. In both, the hero must face evil and his own mortality in order to save the world as he knows it. Both journeys make our hero stronger and he comes out victorious in the end.

In the Major Arcana, our hero is the Fool and he must take a journey that takes him far from home, through peril and tests of his faith, until he finally triumphs over the darkness and finds enlightenment.

The journey of the hero, or the Fool, is our journey as human beings. It is the journey away from our comfort level to places unknown to face our own darkness. We learn about our dual nature of dark vs. light and the constant pull to keep us in the material world instead of the world of the Spirit. In the end, we learn to find balance and harmony and triumph over that which would hold us down. At the end of our journey, we find that we are home again and have been Enlightened along the way.

The Tarot can help us along our journey. It can give us illumination in our darkest hours. It can show us how to deal with whatever life can throw at us. In the journey through the Major Arcana, we find that we are never alone; there is always a Higher Power along with us that we can call on for help. It is only in reaching out to the Divine Help that we can find the Enlightenment that we seek.

But right about now you might be saying to yourself, "Hey, I don't care about all this woo-woo stuff. I just want to do it for fun!" And you know; that is just fine with me. The Tarot absolutely is great fun and with the vast amount of decks on the market, you can rest assured that you will find one or more that you really enjoy and have a wonderful time with.

But don't be surprised if somewhere along the line you begin to have more than just a good time. You just may find that you have unlocked some beauty secrets from the depths of your soul and that suddenly you have become the Fool and have embarked on the greatest journey of your life. And somewhere in the back of your mind, you'll hear my little voice saying, "I told you so!"

SELF HELP AND SELF ASSERTION

Two of the most popular searches on the internet every day of the week is Self-help and self-assertion. Nearly everyone has an inborn desire to help themselves either in a material or spiritual way. Self-help is the most important way of achieving self-acceptance. If you have decided on self-help, or self-assertion techniques as a way to achieve personal development and success, then be very pleased for yourself for taking personal accountability for your shortcomings. You have decided to work on accepting yourself and then improving yourself on the basis of your inherent humanity.

Being a fallible human being, as everyone is, it is really easy to put yourself down from time to time instead of accepting that as a human you are bound to make mistakes. Self-help is about accepting that you have flaws, but you are doing something about them in a positive and assertive way.

Basically being assertive means standing up for yourself, and what you believe, in a nonhostile way. Being assertive is not about applying violence or bullying to get your point of view across. The difference is, when you are being assertive you are still in charge of your actions, but when you are applying violence nearly all of your behavior will be reckless.

The thing is, people are a lot more certain to act in response to your wishes when you are being assertive. This is all because you are talking in a clear calm way - not because they are frightened of your anger. More often than not, your hostility is about winning a disagreement and making the other person agree that you are right. The assertion is not about winning or dominating the other person. No, the assertion is all about getting your point of view across in a clear none aggressive manner.

If you have the inclination to become furious during a disagreement and get verbally or physically aggressive in a short time, give yourself a time out: take a few deep breaths and then count to ten slowly. Hardly anything good has ever come out of a heated argument, so taking a few deep breaths and counting will always work if you want to calm down quickly. Also while doing the breathing and counting remember to think about how everyone has their own opinions and their own shortcomings.

If you accept that everyone is unique and that everyone is special and flawed in equal measure then accepting yourself for what you are will be a lot easier.

WAYS TO WORK ON YOUR SPIRITUAL SELF

True integrity means that we have all four areas of life working in harmony with each other. Our physical self complements and enhances our emotional, mental and spiritual selves. Each dimension complements and enhances the other three. In fact, when you are 'in' integrity, there is no awareness of the four separate selves. There is only "I".

Even though that's true, while we are working towards wholeness and becoming our best self, one of the four areas might get left behind. The way to bring them back in balance is to focus on the 'weaker' side until it is as strong as the others. Here are some thoughts on the spiritual self.

Working on the Spiritual Self

For me, the spiritual self is the part that is most attuned to our connection to God, the Universe, Buddha, whatever we call "That Which Created and Links All of Us".

The spiritual side is the part that is most difficult to connect to as we go through our daily lives. Few of make room for this dimension as we rush off to work, run around town dropping and picking up our kids, getting to the store and getting dinner out on time, spending the requisite hours on the job - and then some, ensuring that we have the basic needs taken care of. Very few of us are strong enough to have enduring faith when we are hungry or exhausted or wondering where we will lay our head down tonight.

01. Schedule your spiritual 'connection'

Because we don't get reminders of our spiritual need in quite the same way as our physical needs (hunger and tiredness, for example), we must stay conscious of that need and take care of it on a regular basis. For most of us, this means planning a set time each day (or multiple times a day) for prayer, meditation or reflection.

02. Feel Your Oneness in Nature

One of the easiest reminders we have of our spiritual connection is right outside your door. Every time you leave your house you come face to face with God's greatest gift to us: the physical world. Whether you are in a rural or urban setting, there are reminders of His grace everywhere in the form of trees, birds, shrubs, weeds, and water. Even in the city, the one thing that cannot be replaced with concrete and steel is the air. The moment we leave the air-conditioned haven of our office building, we encounter air. Take a moment and be grateful for it! It may seem too little or too silly, but it will help you stay connected.

03. Learn to breathe in a spiritual way.

No matter where we are, we can always take three long, slow, deep, conscious breaths. The slower you go, inhaling through the nose and exhaling through the mouth, the calmer you become. Keep your mind wrapped around the process of breathing and you will be amazed at how quickly you feel calm and relaxed. This simple technique brings you quickly to your place of wisdom, the place within you where the connection to God happens. Enjoy it often!

A GUIDE TO FEEDING YOUR SPIRITUAL SELF

"I'm so lonely that I can't stand it." "I just have to accept that I am going to be alone forever." "What's wrong with me? I can't seem to find anyone to love and will love me back?" These are statements that I hear over and over again from the souls on the couch across from me. Emotional pain pours out like beads of sweat on a sweltering day, permeating the room with the smell of despair. Quick glances upward, faint flickers of hope emitting from their eyes as they look to me for help. I know their pain; been there, done that.

For most people, there is nothing more painful than being single when you want to be married or in a committed relationship. After all, it's supposed to be easy, right? You tell yourself that you're a good person; that you want to love someone and have him or her love you back. You wake longing to create a deeply intimate bond with that someone special and live in the land of Happily Ever After. It is the future, not the here and now that will bring happiness and a sense of contentment.

"Why can't I find someone to be in a relationship with?" a young lady ponders.

"What about your relationship with your spiritual self?" I ask.

"I don't give that a lot of thought or attention. I am too busy looking for that one person who will be my soul mate to spend time thinking about that. I don't even know how to think about my spiritual self. And, I don't have the time."

It's curious how people expect to create a great relationship with another person when they don't have a great relationship with their Spiritual Self. Feeding the soul is where the journey to creating a dream relationship starts. It is about the here and now, not a fairy tale of the future. Connecting to mindfulness is an important step in living in the here and now; it starts you on a trek of moving away from pain and toward peace and tranquility.

Mindfulness is the act of observing your moment to moment experience and marinating it in kindness. It is about focusing your attention on what is happening at the moment; what you are feeling and thinking at any moment in time. It is being in a stance of openness, where acceptance and non-judgment allow curiosity to flourish. Being curious is critical, as it puts us in a state of seeking wisdom, one of the more valuable things in the universe (intimacy and deep love being the most valuable).

"Have you ever thought about assessing situations

without tagging on a judgment?" I ask.

"What do you mean?"

"For example, simply saying 'What I'm doing isn't working for me' and stopping there rather than adding on 'because I'm a loser?'"

"No. Not really. Look at my life. It is nothing like I dreamt it would be. I am a loser!"

Assessing without judging is a critical component of mindfulness. It allows us to look at our morals, values, and belief systems from a perspective of what is working and what is not without poisoning the food (thoughts) that we feed our Soul. Judgment is toxic. Non-judgment is nourishing and leads to enlightenment, empowerment, and transformation.

Mindfulness allows us to look at our spiritual Self and provides the opportunity to feed it a nine-course meal. By its very nature, it is an act of self-love and acceptance. It allows us to look for and create validation from within, rather than looking for it from outside sources.

When we create internal validation, we are in a creative stance which we can control. We fuel our spiritual self and create self-love and positive mental states of mind like self-acceptance. We walk with life in our gait and radiate out warmth, which is attractive. It creates connections. When we look for validation from outside sources, we are in a desperate stance, we have no control, and we feed negative mental states of mind like Fear. We walk as if the weight of the world is on our shoulders. It is cold and pushes others away. It creates loneliness.

As you continue on your journey to create a dream relationship, remember to feed your Soul a healthy diet of love, warmth, mindfulness, self-acceptance, and hope and do it from a non-judgmental stance. Make a promise to your spiritual Self that you will never starve it or poison it again with negative thoughts which contain no nutritional value. In doing so, you will radiate and attract others in a way that you have never experienced.

PERSONAL DEVELOPMENT AND SELF HELP

Sometimes, the experts forget they were once beginners. You must be gentle with beginners; they have great potential to be experts. -**Lailah Gifty Akita**

Personal development is a lifelong process. It's a way for people to assess their skills and qualities, consider their aims in life and set goals in order to realize and maximize their potential. It covers activities that improve personal awareness and identity, develop talents and potential, build human capital and facilitate employability, enhance the quality of life ultimately contributing to the realization of dreams and aspirations.

Not limited to self-help, the concept involves formal and informal activities for developing others in roles such as teacher, guide, counselor, manager, life coach or mentor. When personal development takes place in the context of institutions, it refers to the methods, programs, tools, techniques, and assessment systems that support human development at the individual level in organizations.

Personal development includes the following activities:

- Improving self-awareness
- Improving self-knowledge
- Improving skills or learning new ones
- Becoming a self-leader.
- The building or renewing identity/self-esteem
- Developing strengths or talents
- Improving wealth
- Spiritual development
- Identifying or improving potential
- Building employability or (alternatively)

human capital

- Enhancing lifestyle or the quality of life

- Improving health

- Fulfilling aspirations

- Initiating a life enterprise or (alternatively) personal autonomy

- Defining and executing personal development plans (PDPs)

- Improving social abilities

Ways to achieve personal growth:

- **Read a good book (non-fictional) every day** - Books are concentrated sources of wisdom. The more books you read, the more you expose yourself to wisdom.

- **Create an inspirational environment** - Your environment sets the mood and tone for you. If you are living in an inspirational environment, you are going to be inspired every day.

- **Overcome your fears** - All of us have fears. Fear of uncertainty, fear of public speaking, fear of risk. All our fears keep us in the same position and prevent us from growing. Recognize that your fears reflect areas where you can grow. Face your fears squarely. Seek some experts help if required to overcome these fears.

- **Have a fixed exercise routine** - Never compromise on exercise. A fit and the healthy physical body is the first step towards your personal growth

- **Get out of your comfort zone** - Real growth comes with hard work and sweat. Being too comfortable doesn't help us grow - it makes us stagnate. Start trying new things, take on tasks and assignments which you've never done before

- **Stay focused with a to-do list** - Start your day with a list of tasks you want to complete. This will help you to stay focused, and slowly improve your daily productivity. You'll feel better when you're happy with your day's achievements

- **Learn from people who inspire you** - Think about people you admire, people who inspire you. It could be your favorite sportsman, a hard-working entrepreneur, or even your father/mother/brother or friend. These people reflect certain qualities you want to have for yourself too, so try and pick up the good qualities of these people

- **Wake up early** - Early to bed, and early to rise is recommended for good reasons. Rising up early in the morning helps to improve your productivity and your quality of life. You start becoming in tune with nature

- **Stay away from negative people** - Wherever we go, there are bound to be negative people. Don't spend too much of your time around them if you feel they drag you down.

- **Meditate** - Meditation helps to calm you and be more conscious. It has a very balancing effect on you, especially if practiced for a considerable duration.

"Let us wake up and live our life with fulfillment, do our duties with passion, and live with joy."

CHAPTER THREE

BUILD A BETTER RELATIONSHIP WITH YOURSELF AND OTHERS

SCIENTIFIC AND SPIRITUAL MAPS

A couple of years ago we heard about the important work of researcher Dr. John Gottman, who observed thousands of couples in his lab in Seattle, Washington. It was validating to see that his work identified the same important behaviors we had observed, separating couples who did well in therapy from those who decided to end their marriages. We noted several behaviors characteristic of couples in distress. Dr. Gottman calls these behaviors "The Four Horsemen of the Apocalypse": contempt, defensiveness, and stonewalling. We also observed that whatever efforts one partner might make to get out of this pattern, the other partner was likely to foil. We began to refer to this phenomenon as "shooting your foot off." On the other hand, Gottman found that there were seven characteristics of happily married couples. We have learned these behaviors the hard way, through our own personal experiences and previous relationships. In more than twenty-five years of observing couples in therapy, we have noted the presence of the following behaviors. We'll discuss them at length below, but in summary, you will know your marriage is improving when you:

1. enhance your love maps
2. nurture your fondness and admiration
3. turn toward each other instead of away
4. let your partner influence you
5. solve your solvable problems
6. overcome gridlock
7. create shared meaning.

From our studies of Jungian psychology and our belief in a universal set of truths, we were not surprised to learn that these behaviors were the same truths described in spiritual wisdom. We are not theologians; however, we have long had an interest in reading the work of great thinkers in the area of spirituality. Recently we attended a lecture by Dr. Francis Vanderwall, a scholar, on the parables of Jesus. The parallels between the principles in this parable about relationships and those in John Gottman's latest book, The Seven Principles for Making Marriage Work, are striking.

Since our counseling is based upon a practical spirituality, we have been interested in a current research that records in a scientific way what we have known intuitively. The discussion that follows provides a bridge between the valley and transformation. Carl Jung wrote about the self with a small "s" and the Self with a capital "S." The small self refers to our individual ego and life drama. The capital Self refers to our connection with a spiritual reality much greater than ourselves. It is helpful when we tell a couple that what they are going through is experienced by others. It is comforting to think in "S" questions and to look at our reality in a larger context. The poet Rainer Maria Rilke remarked, "We need to learn to love the questions and to live our way to the answers."

Henri Nouwen's book begins with a description of the parable of "The Prodigal Son," which he called "The Story of Two Sons and Their Father." This material provides a clear and beautiful example of asking the "S" questions. It also illustrates Jung's concept of universal wisdom. Many other examples can be found in spiritual tradition. The parable of the Prodigal Son beautifully describes the ability of our soul to turn lead (our mistakes) into gold (transformation).

There was a man who had two sons. The younger one said to his father, "Father, let me have the share of the estate that will come to me." So the father divided the property between them. A few days later, the younger son got together everything he had and left for a distant country where he squandered his money on a life of debauchery. When he had spent it all, that country experienced a severe famine, and now he began to feel the pinch, so he hired himself out to one of the local inhabitants who put him on his farm to feed the pigs. And he would willingly have filled himself with the husks the pigs were eating but no one would let him have them. Then he came to his senses and said, "How many of my father's hired men have all the food they want and more, and here am I dying of hunger! I will leave this place and go to my father and say: "Father, I have sinned against heaven and against you; I no longer deserve to be called your son; treat me as one of your hired men..." So he left the place and went back to his father. When he was still a long way off, his father saw him and was moved with pity. He ran to the boy, clasped him in his arms and kissed him. Then his son said, "Father I have sinned against heaven and against you. I no longer deserve to be called your son." But the father said to his servants, "Quick! Bring out the best robe and put it on him; put a ring on his finger and sandals on his feet. Bring the calf we have been fattening, and kill it; we will celebrate by having a feast because this son of mine was dead and has come back to life; he was lost and is found." And they began to celebrate. Now the elder son was out in the field, and on his way back, as he drew near the house, he could hear music and dancing. Calling one of the servants he asked what it was all about. The servant told him, "Your brother has come, and your father has killed the calf we had been fattening because he has got him back safe and sound." He was angry then and refused to go in, and his father came out and began to urge him to come in; but he retorted to his father, "All these years I have slaved for you and never once disobeyed any orders of yours, yet you have never offered me so much as a kid for me to celebrate with my friends. But, for this son of yours, when he comes back after swallowing up your property-he and his loose women-you kill the calf we had been fattening."

The father said, "My son, you are with me always, and all I have is yours. But it was only right we should and rejoice because your brother here was dead and has come to life; he was lost and is found." Let's compare Gottman's principles for a successful marriage with the compelling parable of "The Prodigal Son." For a more in-depth theological discussion, we recommend Nouwen's book; what we shall examine here are the embedded psychological precepts that validate the theories Carl Jung postulated in Dreams, Memories, and Reflections and in other works, namely that if you remove the obstacles that prevent you from accessing your authentic Self, it will lead you toward a transformed life of the "Truths." In order to demonstrate this, here is a brief comparison between Gottman's work and "The Prodigal Son": John Gottman and the Parable of "The Prodigal Son"

Principle 1: Enhance Your Love Maps

John Gottman found that successful couples have a map of their partner's psychological reality, and understand their partner's interior world. Put poetically: How many loved your moments of glad grace, And loved your beauty with love false or true, But one man loved the pilgrim soul in you, And loved the sorrows of your changing face; William Butler Yeats-from "When You Are Old" In "The Prodigal Son," the father understands his son's pilgrim soul. Even though the son went away and went wild in the valley of the shadows, the father understood his true repentance and was anxious to take him in again. In unsuccessful couples, we see rigidity in a tendency to hang on to past hurts. They do not have a psychological map of one another's complexity, nor are they able to talk about and explore their "pilgrim souls" together. It is significant in "The Prodigal Son," that the father didn't need to hear all his son's explanations, why he had done what he did and how badly he felt. The father already understood this. He had a deep psychological map to his son.

Developing a love map for yourself and your partner is important if you wish to understand your inner self and that of the significant person in your life. It is very difficult to explain who we are if we don't know who we are.

Principle 2: Fondness and Admiration

In successful couples, we observe playful fondness and mutual respect. In "The Prodigal Son" the father's unconditional love and fondness for both of his sons is evident. He, in fact, loves them just the way they are.

Principle 3: Turn Toward Each Other Instead ofAway

Gottman has found that when times are difficult, healthy couples have an ability to turn toward each other and dialogue with their conflict. In "The Prodigal Son," it is significant that the father runs out to meet his returning youngest son. According to Jewish law at the time, a father should never run to meet anyone. The father was less concerned with the rigid laws than he was with the joyful reunion with his son. It was the love that was most important and led to a powerful reconciliation.

Principle 4: Let Your Partner Influence You

In his research with abusive couples, Gottman found that abusers are almost totally incapable of allowing the other's influence. In viewing tapes of couples unable to accept one another's influence, it is not unusual to see an abusive partner discount almost everything that the other says. For example, if one partner says, "The sky is blue," the other may respond, "No it's not; it's blue and red." It's more important to be right than to have love or peace of mind. In the parable of "The Prodigal Son," the father allows himself to be influenced to give his sons their inheritance early. Again, this went against Jewish laws of the time, because fathers did not give an inheritance to a younger son, nor did they give it early. Scott Peck described this kind of love when he said that true love is "to will the good of the other." It is also important that the prodigal son had to repent to his father. In good relationships, people take responsibility for their own behavior. They do not sit and sulk like a child and wait for someone to come to them. We are shown in "The Prodigal Son" that the oldest son is not yet ready to come to the father.

He is caught up in self-righteous thinking. We find this with dysfunctional couples; each feels right and believes the other one should come to beg for forgiveness. Bill demanded perfection and guilt-tripped his wife Sally when she failed to meet his exacting standards. Sally would run away when she felt overwhelmed by Bill's criticism. He blamed her for "refusing to work on the relationship" even when we pointed out that he had missed many more sessions than had his wife. The stress was palpable, and we suggested they take a break from one another. They were able to benefit from separate vacations, and when we next saw them Bill admitted he was too demanding. Sally agreed to discuss issues if the discussions were civil and if Bill would refrain from personal attacks.

Among the ground rules, we established were; -Avoid absolutes like "never" and "always."

- Take turns communicating feelings.

- Moderate your voice and be respectful.

- Listen without interrupting, then verify what you think you heard.

- Acknowledge your partner's feelings and any truth in his or her observations.

- Discuss one subject at a time, and ask permission to change the subject.

- Limit discussions to one hour at most, then schedule follow-up discussions at a mutually agreeable time and place.

Bill and Sally have a long way to go, but they're still talking and trying to understand one another's perspective. Even when you're in the right, it's unlikely your partner will say, "I see that you've been right all along, and I've been a jerk. Can you ever forgive me? From now on, I'll do it your way." Face it that's not going to happen. Be gracious enough to accept your partner's acquiescence without insisting on an abject apology.

Principle 5: Solve Your Solvable Problems

Successful couples can discuss conflicts and accept one another's influence, so they are able to solve most problems together. Sometimes they have to accept that certain problems are not solvable and that they can go on loving each other, respecting their differences while retaining their closeness and joy in one another. In "The Prodigal Son," there is initially an unsolvable problem with the youngest son, so he goes away to learn his lesson. There is also an unsolvable problem with the oldest son, who feels resentful because he has done his duty and is not being rewarded. The difference is that the youngest son learns his lesson, then returns to the father and accepts responsibility for his mistakes. The oldest son pulls away, and the parable ends with his unwillingness to see either his brother's or his father's point of view. It is very significant that the oldest son asks his father why he is having a party for "this son of yours." The father corrects him, referring to "your brother." By so doing, he tries to lead the son toward compassion, toward understanding his brother's point of view. At the end of the parable, the oldest brother is not yet able to do this. He is convinced he is right and is unwilling to consider another point of view. Self-righteousness prevents many couples from reconciling their differences and creating a joyful existence together.

Principle 6: Overcome Gridlock

In order to overcome gridlock, Gottman teaches that couples must learn to support one another's dreams. To do so, we must first understand our dreams and be able to talk about them with each other. The demise of many a marriage has resulted from the inability of one partner to communicate his or her deep dream and the other partner's inability to understand and support it. Marge has been offered a promotion, but it means she'll have to travel, and Fred is afraid she'll find someone else. He secretly hopes she won't get the promotion and in subtle ways undermines her self-confidence. His dream is starting a family, but he cannot admit he'd like a baby for fear of appearing unmanly. Fred wants Marge to read his mind and adopt his dream. Insensitive to one another's dreams, they nevertheless create obstacles to their fulfillment. Sometimes, love means letting go; sometimes it means talking, listening, understanding, compromising, and finding a win-win solution to each impasse. In the parable, the father is able to support his youngest son's dream even though it has immediate tragic consequences. He is able to let his son go to follow his dream. Because it is unselfish, letting go can be the purest form of love. When love returns, as when the prodigal returns, love attains the Second Mountain.

Principle 7: Create Shared Meaning

Happy couples are happy. This may sound obvious, but most people miss the point. In our practice, we have counseled many people who thought of home as a place of strife and who could not imagine what it would be like to be happy at home. Many think they have to go on vacation each year to have shared rituals or joyful times. Their marriages are in survival mode. How sad this is. Healthy couples have many rituals. On our honeymoon, we met a couple celebrating their tenth anniversary. They told us that every month they had a mini-anniversary and would give each other some small gift, such as a cigarette lighter or a handkerchief. We thought this a wonderful idea and adopted it, giving each other a little card on the tenth of each month. "The Prodigal Son" teaches us that God has laid out a banquet for us and, to participate in it, we need to relate to each other with love. Unfortunately, the oldest son chooses self-righteousness over the joyful celebration. He thinks of the attack instead of love. As Henri Nouwen puts it: "The world in which I have grown up is a world so filled with grades, scores, and statistics that, consciously or unconsciously, I always try to take my measure against all the others. Much sadness and gladness in my life flow directly from my comparing, and most, if not all this comparing is a useless and terrible waste of time and energy." People who are hopelessly locked in comparisons and power struggles fail to see that there is an abundance of love and joy for celebrating life on a daily basis. They are their own worst enemies, clinging to the jungle lest their partners find a way out.

"The Prodigal Son" gives us a map to leave our childhood programming and learn to love in mature ways. It is striking that this ancient wisdom is now being documented through the careful and systematic observations of Dr. Gottman. In reviewing Dr. Gottman's seven variables present in couples in long-term happy marriages, it is sometimes helpful to remember the beginning stages of a relationship, when these behaviors were perhaps commonly expressed:

- Love maps refer to a deep understanding of your partner's psychological world.

- Fondness can be demonstrated through affection, admiration, or praise.

- Toward versus away means that successful couples build up an emotional positive bank account when they have difficulties they turn toward each other to work them out. Also, on a day-to-day basis, they have many varied mindful moments where they are connected, sharing jokes, touching each other's arm, and fixing meals together, for example.

- Let Your Partner Influence You refers to respecting your partner's opinions and values. Couples are able to maintain an ongoing friendship through mutual respect.

- Solve Your Solvable Problems refers to the ability of successful couples to learn from experience and benefit from past mistakes.

- Overcome Gridlock-Differences are settled through the ability to dialogue with conflict. - Create Shared Memories refers to the rituals, symbols, family pictures, and occasions that reflect the couple's positive bond and shared history.

HOW TO BUILD A BETTER RELATIONSHIP WITH YOURSELF

"What lies behind you and what lies in front of you, pales in comparison to what lies inside of you."
-Ralph Waldo Emerson

It's funny how we've spent our whole life with ourselves, but sometimes the person in the mirror can be the hardest one to get to know. And it goes without saying that it's difficult to truly appreciate something or someone you don't understand. When building confidence and self-esteem, the single most important thing you can do is to rebuild the internal relationship that you have with yourself. Numbers speak volume and it's difficult for negativity to go up against the positive power of Me, Myself and I.

Before diving into how to get to know yourself better and reconstructing self-trust, it's important to begin by making a commitment to stand by the single person who has a hand in all of your decisions, you. Here is an Affirmation of Inner Beauty taken from The Seeds of Beauty, to remind you of the relationship you must continually build with yourself no matter what your stage in life.

[Speak Your Name],

To you, I will never be a fair weather friend.

When you are afraid, I will give you the courage to step forward,

If ever you make a mistake, I will never lose faith in you.

And when you begin to doubt how beautiful you are, I will remind you.

Today and every day I promise to always stand by you.

You are me. I am you.

I Love You.

Print this affirmation and post it in a visible place within your office or home.

It comes as no surprise that building positive self-esteem starts with getting to know yourself again and this will require that you regularly devote some downtime to spend with yourself. What's your favorite movie, place to visit or song to listen to? Set aside time in your schedule to do these things. Fall in love with who you are by supporting yourself and bringing out the best in you through your interests.

What can action steps can I take to build a better relationship with myself?

When we're on a date and getting to know someone, the first thing we do is ask questions. So why not do the same for yourself? Start by asking yourself the following:

What values are important to me?

What are my dreams for the future?

What makes me afraid?

What do I dislike?

How do I envision myself to be?

The thing that would mean the most to me right now is...

The key is, to be honest in your answers. Pay attention to your likes/dislikes. What things are hardest for you to admit to yourself?

After letting myself down so many times in the past, I struggle with trusting myself. What can I do to reconnect?

Reconnecting to who you are and building a better relationship with yourself begins with forgiveness. We all make mistakes and if you hold your mistakes over your head like a guillotine ready to punish you each time you make a mistake, you do yourself more harm than good. Take a blank sheet of paper and fill in the following sentence:

I forgive myself for...

List out every misstep that has made you angry, every mistake that has made you ashamed, and every mistake that has made you feel less than yourself. With the same kindness that you would show a friend, read each sentence aloud. As you read each sentence, allow yourself to gently let it go and ultimately heal.

LEARN TO FIGHT FAIR

There are many relationships in your life. You have a relationship with your family, with your friends, with your co-workers, with people you know and others. No matter how close people are, there are times when arguments happen. But some people do not fight fair, which damages and even destroys relationships.

Why is it important to fight fair?

In an argument, there are two or more people involved and emotions are high. Someone may do something that is not fair and things will start growing spiraling out of control. It could be that one of the arguers has never learned to fight fair.

Keep arguments private.

This means do not fight in public, nor try to bring others into the argument. If someone wants to fight in public this means they want an audience for some reason.

Stay on topic.

If the fight is about not being at a family function, then keep to that subject. Other issues, things from the past are not part of the fight.

Clarify the topic.

What is the true topic of the fight? If you are the one presenting the argument make certain you are fighting over the right matter. When your friend asks for help do not get into a fight over that when the problem is she was not there when you asked for help. If someone has an argument with you, clarify. Make certain you know, it may not be what you thought.

Do not call each other names.

Name calling is not appropriate. This is not limited to unprintable names, this includes calling the other person stupid, idiot, liar, cheater. These words may be said in anger when they are not true. To the other person, these names take hold in their mind.

Do not exaggerate.

Always and never are exaggerations. These are comments that are designed to attack rather than communicate.

Remember respect.

Do not attack. Do not go after a weak spot. "Well, that's why X happened (s) to you" is not appropriate. Your temper may be heating up, but this does not mean you should not respect the other person.

Do not assume.

You do not know what the other person is or was thinking. You do not know what they were feeling. It could be they were worried about something else when you thought they forgot.

Do not yell or scream.

Things can get out of control quickly.

Know when to end the fight.

If things get ugly then the fight needs to end. Stop talking. Stop arguing. Walk away. Announce "We both need to be calm." If the other person starts attacking, stay calm.

Be willing to disagree.

People do not always agree. We have different views,

different ideas, different feelings, and temperaments.

Make it a win/win.

This does not mean winning at all costs. This means to find a compromise. Agree to disagree. Agree to forget about the matter. You both should walk away feeling not embittered, instead, you should feel resolved.

BUILDING BETTER RELATIONSHIPS WITH PEOPLE CLOSE TO YOU

"It is nobler to give yourself completely to one individual than it is to labor for the salvation of the masses".Dag Hammarskjold once said

This is a very powerful truth - it often takes more courage and strength of character to build and repair a relationship with someone really important to you than it does to work for hundreds of strangers who will never know you intimately. Understanding some of the principles behind this statement will help you to build better relationships with people who are important to you.

One of the greatest difficulties encountered today is the break up of what should be close relationships -

marriages turning into divorce, dysfunctional families, businesses torn apart by the strife between the leaders of the business. Very often the people who are unsuccessful in forming such relationships are successful in other aspects of their lives. They are valued members of the community, putting in endless hours to benefit a community organization, they establish good working relationships with colleagues at work. Yet they are failing when it comes to building those really critical relationships.

Identify the important relationships

What are the relationships that are important to you? Your parents, your spouse, your children, your business partner... There will be a list and it is likely to be fairly small. Once you are clear on the important relationships, you need to set aside some time for them. This can be on a daily or weekly basis, a time where you can make positive deposits into their emotional bank account. Some of the time should also be spent thinking about the quality of your relationship. Are there areas of strain? Can you foresee problems ahead?

See problems as opportunities

If the other person is encountering some difficulties in their own life, this could be a great opportunity for you to help that person. Your help could be something as simple as just listening, it could involve offering constructive advice or it could be something even more tangible - you doing something to help out. Of course, this will only really work when you are not in it for your own gain. You must approach this with the attitude of being completely focused on the needs of the other person.

Don't leave issues to grow into mountains

When you find that some problem is occurring in one of your important relationships you need to resolve it with the other person. This can be one of the most difficult things you will have to do in your life. Unfortunately, because we are all individuals with different needs and approaches to life, it is something that you will almost inevitably have to do one or more times in all of your important relationships.

It is very important that you don't let the problem turn into a catastrophe. You need to find the courage in yourself to face up to the problem. Often the things that seem most frightening are the possibilities of completely losing the relationship or losing some of your own self-importance. You need to approach the other person with no attachment to a specific outcome and with the attitude that whatever happens, it's going to be OK in the long run.

Very often, you will find that the other person will welcome your approach as they have sensed the same problem. They will be pleased that you have taken the initiative. Now you both need to be prepared to invest the time to restore a better balance. Be prepared to jointly face up to the issues that are underlying the problem and work out a solution that is acceptable to both of you.

This success quote reveals that one of the greatest challenges we face as human beings is to form deep and meaningful relationships with the small number of people who are most important to us. It's often easier to be a 'public' success, liked by large numbers of people. Developing and building close relationships is critical to us all as human beings, following the guidelines in this chapter for dealing with the inevitable bumps in the road can help you greatly.

SELF IMPROVEMENT WILL BUILD A BETTER RELATIONSHIP

The greatest gift you can give to somebody is your own personal development. Stop waiting for the "someday" that never seems to come. Stop waiting for people and circumstances to change. Instead change what you can, yourself. Don't settle for less than you can be. Strive to be your best self. When you take better care of yourself, everybody wins. You will be a better partner and for that matter, a better parent, a better friend, and a better citizen. Everybody benefits from your personal development.

This may sound a little odd but always work harder on yourself than you do your job. You can change the word "job" to any other area of responsibility such as your marriage or your children. I'm not telling you to go to work tomorrow and put your feet up on your desk with your hands behind your head. If you do, then your supervisor will firmly ask you, "What do you think you're doing?" I don't think your boss will appreciate it if you respond, "I'm just taking care of myself today." What I am telling you to do is to take better care of yourself mentally, physically, emotionally, and spiritually.

Self-responsibility is the goal here, not selfishness. You are not trying to be first but rather the best that you can be. You are taking care of yourself for the people that you love. It's like the pregnant mother who quits smoking for the sake of her unborn child. Or the grandfather who starts an exercise and nutrition program because he wants to watch his grandchildren grow up. By taking better care of us, others will benefit. This can also be compared to keeping your car tuned up. The tune-ups will get you better mileage and the engine will last much longer.

Your decision to improve is the starting point. Decide to take charge of your life TODAY! Decide to separate yourself from the crowd that only makes excuses for why they aren't living life to the fullest. Their excuses are based on fear. You must conquer your fears. If you listen to your fears, you will never know your truest potential. Your fears will act as roadblocks that keep you from experiencing all of the good things that life has to offer. Fear can fill your mind with thoughts that will hold you back. These thoughts may be such as, "I can't", "It's been tried before", "It's too hard" and "I'm not good enough". It doesn't take much of this before you no longer trust your instincts. All of us have been through trials of many kinds. It's not whether you get knocked down; it's whether you get back up. Your past doesn't predict your future. Don't be afraid to live. I challenge you to respond positively, not negatively, to the things that happen to you.

When it looks like you've exhausted all of the possibilities, remember this "You Haven't"! Don't wish for fewer problems, wish for more skills. Surround yourself with people and resources that have the answers for self-improvement. If you have a weakness, you need to be strong enough to admit it and then get some help to correct it. Commit yourself to at least fifteen to thirty minutes per day of study for self-improvement. This can be reading, listening to a tape, or watching a program but make sure you get your time in. You can miss a meal but don't miss this time of the study. Focus on topics that promote spiritual, emotional, physical, and mental growth. Life will become much easier as you become better equipped to handle its challenges.

What could you do with your life if you really decide to? How do you want to be remembered? Stay away from the dead-end street of comparing yourself to others. Doing your best is more important than being the best. Choose to make the most of each and every day. By building a solid foundation of self-improvement you will have so much more to offer to the ones you love. When you are your best self everybody wins.

BARRIERS TO BUILDING A GREAT RELATIONSHIP WITH YOUR FAMILY

What do all effective families have in common? They all have members who love, like, respect and trust each other. The key to having these things in a family is the quality of the relationship each has with the others. In other words, they have great relationships with each other.

If you don't have them in your family then you'd need to build better relationships with each of your family member. This is easier said than done since the challenge of modern families is that everyone is too busy. Everyone has their own schedule. Mum and dad are busy working and the children have their schooling and extra activities like sport and creative arts activities to attend.

Each Person Doing Their Own Thing

Not only is each person busy, but they are also doing it on their own even when they are all at home. Once mum, dad, and the kids are at home, they will each go to their own corner of the house and separately go about their business.

For example, you might find dad on the couch

reading or watching television, mum might be at the computer surfing the internet, the older child might be on the Xbox, PlayStation or some other electronic game while another child might be messaging friends on the smartphone.

If this sounds like your family then you'd need to set aside a time to do something together. It could be on the weekend or weeknights. It could be as short as half an hour or as long as the whole day.

The main thing is to find an agreed upon time to, at least, spend quality time together doing the same activity. Be strict about it. Everyone has to attend. No opt out and no excuses are acceptable.

No One Can Relate to the Others

The second barrier to great relationships is a disconnection. The family does not share anything in common except that they live in the same house. Each person is like a planet revolving around the sun, never meeting except on the rare occasion of an eclipse when the planets align (maybe for dinner?).

If you don't have a shared experience then how can you create shared memories? When your children are older are they able to say, "We had fun doing that!" or "What great times we've had!"? Will there be fond memories or avoid when everyone looks back?

To create fond memories you'd need to find

something fun to do together as a family. It could be simple things like playing games, doing puzzles and cooking together or more elaborate like camping, learning a new skill or doing community service. The important thing is that the family can have fun doing it together.

Family Fun Activities

Decide on which fun activity your family is going to do together and when you're going to do it. Everyone can sit down and brainstorm ideas then you can go through each one and decide the ones that you'd like to do.

CHAPTER FOUR

TACKLE ANXIETY HEAD-ON

ANXIETY IS A CHOICE

Firstly let me congratulate you on your ability to create this state called anxiety. This is uniquely your function. Not everyone can do this, however, you have and now you want to 'get rid of it'. The question I would ask of you is... "Are you sure?" because you have invested a lot of your time in it as well as many other people's time and attention to 'your anxiety problems'. If you were to get rid of it, then what would you put in its place, if anything? So, are you sure that you want to take away this piece of the unique YOU out of your system?. How much of your world have you invested already in this malady you now want to get rid of? What would you do with your new freedom from anxiety if it were to go? That anxiety, at whatever level, is there for a reason - and we will be looking at that in a moment - and this reason must be stronger than your feeling psyche for it to exist as an on-going force within the unique you. So let us look some levels of anxiety, such as: "Mum there's a great big spider in my bedroom" cries a child and the child gets anxious about the spider, a specific creature she imagines can hurt her. Anxiety always relates to hurt. This is controllable anxiety, get rid of the spider equals getting rid of the anxiety, (carefully looking to see there are no other spiders lurking there). I would call this third-line-anxiety. Learned anxiety, overcome with reason and action. This anxiety is a learned one, where the growing person has learned that certain things can harm us and being little (in psyche if not body) there is a need for immediate help from others perceived as being stronger than the self. This is usually enough and can be used in a creative and useful manner. An example would be learning self-defense to ward off bullies at school. There is also the chronic worrier who perceives their worry as an anxiety state, and rightly so, we may say anxiety at a lesser level. I would call this second-line anxiety. Overcome with specific understanding of the self. This is also reasonably easy to overcome by getting to know who you really are. This is not as hard as you may think.

However, there is also another anxiety, of varying degrees, one where it 'takes over' the emotions and won't go away. A terrifying emptiness of blackness filled with 'spiders' of our deep inner psyche's creation, not simply one in the bedroom that can be overcome by a bit of reason, muscle and mum's trusty broom. I would call this first-line anxiety. This is often very difficult to clear, not because it can't be cleared but by the very nature of distrust on which all anxiety is founded. Anxiety is a very real but unconscious form of expression of the hurting child

Let's understand where anxiety comes from. This may be a bit heavy, but stay in there and you'll be supplied with information you need to give you a foundation of knowledge to underpin your new, productive actions. You see, all life must express itself in its own way. You are a special part of that life and you have been since you were first united as one by the penetration of daddy's sperm into mummy's egg. The life they created was a NEW and powerful life. Very different from the first two living creatures (egg and sperm) and already eager to get stuck into life into mummy's womb where it forms into another new life (life meeting life again). Then you grow into a baby, and all the experiences of the mother as she carries you are recorded in your little psyche. Then you are born. What an experience! Life (baby) meeting life (the world baby will live in).

Here is how it ideally works:

Essentially the growing baby wants a mother's attention at all times. Baby has already gone through the amazing life series of development of all the organs of the body and has broken from being dependent on the mother, has traveled the sometimes very scary birth canal and is eager to go on to new things. All this at an emotional level. Then baby goes through a series of transitional developments... firstly the need for acceptance. This is the prime essential and we all carry that through life to the grave. From acceptance baby moves to Being. A genuine, real little bundle of life that his father as a guarantee of strength and mother as an assurance of sustenance, both vital to the growing child. Then with mother and father there to sustain life as a right, the baby moves to what can be called Wellbeing. From there on to Identification where baby identifies with the mother to gain his personal identity and from father for his social identity. Further development for the well-parented child leads to Status as a person and then on to Production.

But what if there is a blockage somewhere along that ideal chain? What if the mother does NOT come when called upon by the baby's very real needs? What would happen if the normal cycle was BLOCKED, for whatever reason, at the first stage when mother was NOT there to supply her loving acceptance/sustenance? The inner pain can be endured for a time, but then the baby may feel that mother will never come and panic starts to become a pathway within the developing psyche. This pathway has no name as it's an indefinable feeling, but it's REAL to baby and it starts to develop its own pathways within the psyche. There starts to despair, hopelessness and the ability to wait for the second stage of BEING by mother's coming is weakened. Infantile death! Baby doesn't know this of course, and it's all pushed into the feeling unconscious to be drawn on at any time later in life when similar experiences are presented.

Here is the foundation of hopelessness, the substance for anxiety.

Let me give you an illustration:

A lady came to me with terrible anxiety about money. She was single, attractive, intelligent. Money was a terrifying agent for her anxiety on a large scale, permeating all she did. However, her older brother was a millionaire by age 21! Same parents, same parental love shared by both. Both accepted. What was the difference? It appeared that her father was a very successful businessman in a middle eastern country. His livelihood was taken away from him by antagonistic government action. The very lives of the father, mother, and son were seriously at risk so they fled to Australia as immigrants with absolutely no money at all. The mother was devastated at all this and my client was conceived during this calamitous period. She wore her mother's grief (loss of livelihood) mother's desperation (lack of money) mother's shame (social scorn) and now mother's contribution to poverty (becoming pregnant) In Australia, the father resumed his business talents and again became wealthy, the son following dad's social example, but the girl only knew, among all the love shared in the family, the distress that associated with money. The son felt prosperity. That was HIS inner picture. The girl felt poverty-anxiety. THAT was her inner picture. She was able to step out of that state with the adult mind of CHOICE leaving behind the anxiety-feeling mind of the inner CHILD.

I will show you how you can do that also a little later.

At each stage of acceptance, being, wellbeing, identification, status, productivity, varying degrees of blocking can take place, leaving behind its legacy of anxiety. Here is first line trauma. Bearing in mind that we are a complex of genetics, ego strength, ancestral and cellular memories, and family dynamics so it would be difficult indeed for a therapist to get to the bottom of it all.

So let's look at the basics of anxiety and as we go if you feel (note the word feel) something stirring within you, take note of it, maybe write it down for your attention later on.

We are a complex of many ingredients and all of these ingredients and circumstances join together to make the strength of our ego (whom we believe ourselves to be). If a person has a strong ego they will act accordingly and if a weak ego (or none at all) they will act accordingly. Makes sense. But for the growing child, the sense of power lies in the parenting, especially mother. So the little ego will react to the bad as well as the good in its own strength. This is why you are unique. No one is the same as you and YOU have the inner answer to your inner anxiety.

Let's look at how it can operate:

Baby can, and does, suffer from mental anguish at the loss of BEING through the loss of mother's attention, for whatever reason, (don't go blaming mum as it quite often, indeed almost always, someone else messing up her routine with baby) and this results in dread sometimes with rage attached and sometimes beyond rage with depressions as a result. Different babies, different ego-responses. What happens, in this case, is baby develops a feeling, nay, a TERROR of the death of the spirit. Baby (you and me) has been through

The joys and energetic drives of LIFE! LIVING! Taking LIFE as LIFE itself with all of the energetic joys of getting 'stuck into life' in mother's endometrium. BLISS! And now being denied this feeling of LIFE! and an emerging sense of DEATH! This once LIFE! being somehow blocked and this blocking taking away that BEING so essential to baby's growth - a growth that cannot be stopped except by death. So: delusional fears of death (self or close persons). Being preoccupied with impending death. Doom. Disaster. Hell. So with this mindset, there is an entry into a panic state, intense apprehension, ANXIETY as first-line anxiety.

A sense of despair 'takes over'. Various phobias are revealed that are peculiar to the experiences of the little baby/child. The ability to wait for 'the good' to come in the form of some accepting person is almost nil. The BEING is challenged by a feeling of separation that will never be satisfied. Therefore no sustenance. Hopelessness called anxiety. This feeling was once REAL and the feeling is still REAL to the inflicted person. However, note that it is a FEELING and as such cannot harm you in any way. A harmless but intense feeling that simply 'takes over' as it did when the baby was experiencing the FACT of non-BEING.

Anxiety at this level can lead to endless talking about their terrible plight. Feeling 'locked in' to endless bad relationships. Difficult to maintain true friendships, which fuels anxiety. Shutting one's self off from help. Isolated by others. More anxiety.

CBT FOR ANXIETY

All of us feel anxious from time to time and in certain situations. It is a normal and natural emotion and can be useful as a stimulus to action. Unfortunately, some of us feel excessively anxious in inappropriate situations, and this is not only unpleasant but can be a serious handicap in our lives.

Anxiety is part of the "Fight or Flight" response to perceived danger, a physiological reflex seen in a huge number of animals. This response physically prepares the animal to fight or run away from danger - it is a survival mechanism and a very effective and successful one at that.

The basic physical mechanism underlying the response is a sudden release of the hormone adrenalin from the adrenal glands (situated on top of the kidneys). This hormone then rushes through the blood and around the body, acting on various organs and muscles to create the all too familiar physical sensations of anxiety - racing heart, breathlessness, dry mouth, flushed skin, dizziness, butterflies in the stomach, nausea, weak legs, trembling limbs, etc. These sensations, which most people (but interestingly, not all!) find unpleasant and frightening, are actually side-effects of the body gearing up for fighting or running away. The racing heart pumps more blood to allow the muscles to work better, the fast breathing brings in more oxygen, etc.

All of this is fine and good if your anxiety is based on a real physical threat - if you've got a lion taking a close interest in you, for example. Fortunately for most human beings, this would be an unusual event! Our "dangers" are rarely physical these days - they're more likely to be the "danger" of failing an exam, or the "danger" of embarrassing yourself in front of others. Indeed, many of our "dangers" don't even exist at all - they are purely in our heads. The "danger of perhaps, maybe, or what-if the lift breaks down and I'm stuck" or the "danger of my anxiety causing me to have a heart attack or pass out".

Cognitive Behavioural Therapy (CBT) views anxiety (and all emotions) as the interaction of three areas of human experience - cognition (our thoughts and mental imagery), physical sensations (what we feel in or with our bodily senses such as feeling hot or short of breath), and behaviour (what we actually do with our bodies such as move in certain ways and interact with others and our environment).

These three areas - thoughts, sensations, behaviors - act together to make up an emotion. For example, when we feel anxious we will typically have certain anxious thoughts ("I'm going to collapse", "I can't stand it"), anxious sensations (nausea, wobbly legs) and anxious behaviors (we rush out of the room, we grab on to someone).

These three areas are linked to one-another in feedback loops. This means that if our physical sensations of anxiety increase, then typically we will experience more frequent and pressing anxious thoughts, and the desire (indeed desperation) to engage in anxious behaviors will increase. This increase in anxious thoughts and behaviors than "loops" or "feeds-back" to increase our anxious physical sensations which then...well, you get the picture. A vicious cycle is set up where we simply get more and more anxious until (usually) we run away from whatever triggered the anxiety in the first place.

This sounds a problem, but actually, this is great news! The fact that the three components of anxiety interact and affect one another allows us to "access" the system and change it for the better!

How do we do this? By targeting those areas of the system over which we have (at least some!) conscious control - our thoughts and our behaviors. We can, to a greater or lesser extent, control or decide what to think. And we can, to an even greater extent, control or decide how to behave. Contrast this with trying to control your heart rate or your blood pressure - much trickier (though I wouldn't say impossible...)

The theory of CBT for anxiety is that by controlling and reducing my anxious thoughts and behaviors I can provide "negative (or inhibitory) feedback" to the system, causing my physical sensations of anxiety to reduce. A reduction in anxious physical sensations will decrease my anxious thoughts and behaviors, which will then, in turn, decrease my anxious physical sensations, and so on. We've set up the opposite of a "vicious cycle" (a "virtuous cycle"?) and our anxiety fades away.

So much for the theory - what about the actual techniques and work involved? As you may have guessed, we can approach the problem of anxiety from two angles - we can tackle anxious thoughts and we can tackle anxious behaviors. In fact, CBT therapists will usually tackle both simultaneously, though the emphasis may be more on thoughts than behavior or vice verse. In my experience, it is helpful to focus more on anxious thoughts when anxiety is a result of thinking about a future event such as exams or an interview. On the other hand, tackling anxious behaviors is the priority in anxiety related to social situations, enclosed spaces or heights, etc - situations that are easily replicated by the client and therapist.

Taking anxious thoughts first. People who experience severe and frequent bouts of anxiety often exhibit what CBT therapists call "Thinking Errors". That is, their thoughts (and indeed their "ways of thinking") are unrealistic and unhelpful, making their anxiety worse, and even being the initial cause of the anxiety in the first place.

Examples of common Thinking Errors in anxiety are "Fortune Telling" (thinking that you know what is going to happen in the future) and "Catastrophising" (assuming the worst possible scenario will come to pass): "I will fail the interview and never get a good job" or "I will pass out and my colleagues will laugh". Thoughts like these will obviously increase person anxiety.

We tackle these thoughts by challenging them, questioning them, and asking them to back themselves up with evidence. It's a Court of Law for these thoughts and they're charged with Irrationality! How can you see into the future? How do you know that you will fail the interview? Have you always failed every interview you've ever done? or How do you know you will pass out? Have you passed out every other time you've been in that situation?

Or we can take a slightly different tack and question their assumptions of what will happen if things do in fact go poorly. What if you do happen to fail the interview? What will happen? Does everyone who fails an interview end up on the scrap heap? Is that what you'd tell a friend who'd failed an interview? or What if you do pass out? What will happen? Will your colleagues really laugh? Or will they be concerned for you?

By questioning our anxious thoughts we can stop simply assuming they're right and begin to look for alternative ways of thinking about the situation. For example, you might remember that in fact, you've always done pretty well in interviews in the past, or that a friend failed an interview for one job only to land an even better one a while later. So you might think instead that "Actually I've got a fair chance of doing OK in this interview, and even if I don't get this job it's not the end of the world". This thought is not only more balanced and realistic, but it will also diminish your anxiety.

Anxious behaviors are the behaviors that we consciously choose to do (or not to do!) as a result of our anxiety - they are NOT the physical sensations of anxiety (these aren't under our immediate control). We engage in these behaviors in an attempt to reduce and alleviate our anxiety. There are two overlapping classes of anxiety-related behaviors. There are so-called "Safety Behaviours", such as sitting down or grabbing hold of something when you feel anxious and dizzy. And there are "Avoidance Behaviours", such as excluding yourself from social gatherings.

These behaviors seem to work in the short term - you're fear of passing out diminishes, and you completely avoid the anxiety of the works do. But you're storing up problems in the longer term. You'll start to believe that you HAVE to sit down when you feel anxious or you WILL DEFINITELY pass-out, and the next time you're invited to a social gathering you will be even more anxious.

Safety Behaviours prevent you from learning to cope with your anxious sensations, and Avoidance Behaviours prevent you from challenging your anxious thoughts.

There's no denying that the physical sensations of anxiety can be unpleasant, but they are temporary and are not life-threatening. A racing heart, weak legs, nausea, and light-headedness aren't fatal. But they can feel certainly feel like it, so the way to prove to yourself that you won't die or pass out or throw up or whatever it is you're worried about is to go out and get yourself some anxiety!

Deliberately putting yourself in your anxiety-provoking situations (crowded shop, tall building, whatever) is the first step to recovery. You can do this in a "graded" way (i.e. start with less busy shops or less tall buildings) before moving on to bigger challenges. Or you can "go in at the deep end" and expose yourself to your worst nightmare. And you just stay there - in the shop or observation deck - and you refuse to do any Safety Behaviours. If you feel dizzy when you feel dizzy, but you refuse to hold on to anything. If you feel nauseous, you just let yourself feel nauseous. Remember: these sensations are side effects of adrenalin and will not harm you. Many people even find them pleasurable - hence roller-coasters and bungee-jumping!

And then you just stay there some more. And some more. And then a bit more. Your anxiety will probably be huge to start with. You'll get the whole lot - feeling sick, feeling faint, feeling that your chest will explode, your mind is mind racing, " I've got to get out of here!", your legs seeming about to take you away anyway, etc. But if you just stick with it - not fighting it but just "experiencing it" - you'll find things start to change. It can take anything from a few minutes to even an hour, but eventually, your anxiety will wane. It's almost as if you get bored with being anxious! Here you are, all het-up and ready to go, and nothing happening. Indeed, in a way, your body does get bored. After all, there's only so much adrenalin that your body can produce at any one time, and if it's not really needed (i.e. your not running from a lion) then it'll stop making it. And less adrenalin means less anxious physical sensations.

By staying in your anxiety-provoking situation you give yourself a chance to "habituate" to it - you have become used to it. This is an incredibly powerful thing to do. Not only have you faced up to your fears but you have proven to yourself that anxiety is bearable. Unpleasant, yes, but temporary and non-fatal. Your anxious thoughts about dying or passing out are shown to be wrong.

So what do you do now? Well, as you may have guessed, you go out and do it again. And again. And again. The more you enter into - AND STAY - in your anxiety-provoking situations, the better you'll become at coping with your anxiety. You (and your body) will stop fearing these situations and, eventually, they will fail to produce any anxiety in you.

ANXIETY AND RELATED DISORDERS

If you're sitting in a tornado shelter feeling apprehension about a tornado warning on the radio, then you probably have a normal fear response to your circumstances. If you're sitting in there on a clear day, trembling, sweating and feeling doomed, then you probably have an anxiety disorder. Webster's Dictionary defines anxiety as "An abnormal and overwhelming sense of apprehension and fear with physiological signs such as shortness of breath, a rapid pulse, or chest pain." Anxiety Disorders are one of the most common psychiatric conditions, affecting fifteen to twenty percent of the general population.

The first order of business for a physician evaluating anxiety is to determine as accurately as possible the patient's complete state of health. At least one-third of patients with an underlying organic disorder present with anxiety symptoms. These could include too much thyroid hormone, problems with the adrenal glands, an unrecognized heart disorder, or diabetes. Treatment of the underlying medical problem thereby becomes the primary treatment for the anxiety.

The second order of business is to determine if a patient is putting something into their body which is causing the anxiety. This could include alcohol, which is a frequent cause of a cycle of anxiety. Other substances which could cause anxiety would be stimulants like diet pills, amphetamines or cocaine. Finally, some prescription drugs do not mix well together, especially when they are broken down by the same enzymes in the liver, and may cause severe anxiety. There are certain herbal remedies such as yohimbine (a purported male enhancer), which in some individuals, can cause anxiety. Elimination of these substances is the treatment for this type of anxiety, so a patient needs to be forthright about all substances and prescriptions which he is taking.

A type of primary anxiety disorder is the panic attack. This is usually unexpected, peaks in about ten minutes and usually lasts less than an hour. It is characterized by a feeling of losing control or going crazy, trembling or shaking, profuse sweating or chills or hot flashes, rapid heart rate, and a sense of not being able to catch one's breath. It may be associated with agoraphobia, which is a fear of being trapped or unable to escape. (Agoraphobia can occur by itself, and thus be considered as another form of primary anxiety.)

There is another form of anxiety which most often begins in childhood. It is the fear of separation from an important attachment figure, for example, a parent. This leads to a form of anxiety called separation anxiety which can occur at later times in life when one is faced with losing another attachment figure.

Some anxiety sufferers have an inordinate fear of humiliation in social or performance situations. Once again it is the physical symptoms which define the condition. One could be tormented by flushing (or blushing), rapid heart rate, shortness of breath, and/or a sense of doom. If it is a fear of social situations it is called Social Anxiety or phobia; fear of performance humiliation is called Performance Anxiety.

Some anxiety sufferers can have symptoms brought on by a specific object or situation. These are called the various and sundry phobias. It might be the fear of heights, fear of crossing a bridge, fear of spiders or germs. Again it is the intense emotional and physical symptoms which make this form of anxiety so disabling.

Another form of anxiety is Obsessive-Compulsive Disorder. A person suffering from this may perform certain rituals to allay the anxiety. This could include excessive hand-washing, not stepping on cracks in the sidewalk, or repetitively locking and relocking a door. Jack Nicholson played an Obsessive-Compulsive in a movie a few years ago (Melvin Udall in "As Good As It Gets"), which very poignantly portrayed the interpersonal difficulties which can occur secondary to this condition. Dustin Hoffman's "Rain Man" portrayed a Tourette's Syndrome/Autistic patient's extreme dependence on rituals to alleviate mounting anxiety.

If a person has six months or more of constant generalized anxiety and excessive worry with the physical and emotional repercussions of anxiety, this is called Generalized Anxiety Disorder. Sometimes this particular spectrum of symptoms can be secondary to a mood disorder such as depression or manic-depression. In this latter case, treatment would be for a mood disorder.

There is an anxiety disorder which occurs after a person has endured a shocking situation in which he has faced the possibility of his own death. We see this in soldiers who have been traumatized on the battlefield. It can occur after a terrible accident or a natural disaster. The person has panic attacks and vivid nightmares. This type of anxiety is called Post-Traumatic Stress Disorder. The VA Hospital system has developed an extensive body of knowledge about this disorder and various specific techniques for treating it. Adjustment Disorder is a much less intense form of anxiety than PTSD. In this situation, an individual develops anxiety secondary to a new situation such as a new job or a different family arrangement.

Treatment of anxiety usually involves both psychological and medical treatment. Identifying sources of anxiety and likewise identifying physical symptoms can eliminate some of the dread ones has for intermittent anxiety. Sometimes with phobias, there can be supportive desensitization which can help alleviate symptoms. Medications can include anti-anxiety agents such as diazepam or clonazepam, but care has to be taken to avoid medication dependency. The SSRI antidepressants like fluoxetine have anti-anxiety properties as well. Tricyclic antidepressants like clomipramine can be used to treat anxiety but have a greater incidence of side-effects.

SOCIAL ANXIETY DISORDER

Social anxiety is the fear of being judged by others in social situations. In reality, this is not happening, and the sufferer of social anxiety knows this to be the case, but the unconscious part of the brain thinks it is happening and the stressful feelings stay present.

It takes hard work to overcome social anxiety, but it can be done. But you need to tackle to issue head-on and not feel sorry for yourself. This article will discuss social anxiety, in general, to help you learn the truth. Towards the end of the article a no-nonsense, no mumbo-jumbo approach to overcoming anxiety is highlighted.

People with the disorder are afraid that they will embarrass themselves in front of an audience. Sometimes anxiety can actually progress into a panic attack. Because of this, the person who suffers from the disorder will become very uncomfortable in any kind of social situation or will even start to avoid social situations altogether.

Anxiety changes the way of your thinking from positive rational thoughts to irrational and negatively exaggerated beliefs about social settings in general and the negative opinions of others. It can interfere with everyday life and the relationships you form.

People with a less severe form of the disorder may be afraid of a specific public situation, such as public speaking. But in most cases, the disorder covers many different situations such as eating, social gatherings, and even using a public restroom (this condition is also known as paruresis and a link to my paruresis blog is given at the end of the article).

The disorder could be connected to other social issues, such as panic attacks, OCD and depression. In fact, a lot of people with social anxiety first seek help with complaints related to these other disorders.

Tackling anxiety alone may be difficult. It is better to get help from support groups and friends. Professional treatment and advice from a doctor are required. The last thing you should do is sit at home and feel sorry for yourself. That way the anxiety wins. You need to be strong, ask for help, and take positives steps to overcome your anxiety.

OVERCOMING ANXIETY WITH SELF IMPROVEMENT

Personal growth to overcome anxiety is the power to change your life. A life of panic and anxiety is no way to live.

If the symptoms of this hindering, fear-driven behavior have been preventing you from being and doing all that you desire, then read on to discover some helpful tips. It is possible to overcome and be in charge of your life and stop letting fear, anxiety, and stress have control.

7 Successful Tips to Swiftly Overcome Anxiety:

1.) CALL ON GOD - This tip has been listed first because God should always be first in our lives. The moment something else takes first place is the moment we allow the disorder to spread in our lives. Pray and call on God daily.

God says He will never leave you, so you can boldly say, "The Lord is my helper, I will not fear what man can do." (Hebrews 13:6)

2.) GUARD YOUR MIND & HEART - What you allow into your mind long enough is eventually going to get into your heart and show up in your life. Watch closely what you put in your mind and make sure it is positive.

Are you watching and listening to news, music, and movies with crude, fear-driven, disturbing, negative, and stressful messages? Then you are allowing this garbage into your mind. Would you allow a garbage truck to unload in your house?

"Keep your heart with all diligence, for out of it spring the issues of life." - Proverbs 4:23

3.) DAILY MEDITATION & AFFIRMATIONS
- This follows the second tip. After putting a stop to negative intake, that encourages fear and anxiety, you now need to replace it with positive, confidence building thoughts, images, and words.

No one can preach to you as you can preach to you. Renew your mind daily. Take time to daily meditate and affirm positive confidence building statements to build yourself up.

Start with positive affirmations such as the following. I am bold, courageous, confident, and powerful. I am proud of myself for the positive changes I am making daily. God has given me a spirit of power, love, and a sound mind.

4.) HEALTHY LIFESTYLE - A healthy lifestyle is critical to your total well being. You are spirit, mind, and body. It is impossible to let one area of your being go downhill and not have it affect you.

A healthy, balanced diet that reduces sugar, alcohol, and caffeine will reduce stress and anxiety levels. An exercise routine, even one of simply taking regular walks, will quickly help lift your spirits.

5.) BE AWARE OF YOUR INNER DIALOGUE - What type of conversation is going on in your head? Do you speak to yourself with kindness, respect, and love; like you would with someone you care about?

Stop rehearsing your past failures, shortcomings, and mistakes over and over. Let them go and acknowledge that you have the ability to change your present and future. Make a list of your positive qualities and abilities. Then remind yourself of them. Speak to yourself as if you were your own best friend.

6.) TACKLE FEAR HEAD ON - We've all experienced the fear and panic that can overtake you with no notice. Fear is a thief and it steals our destinies and prevents our progress. It causes those who should be bold and aggressive to shrink back and be timid.

Do not let fear control you. Face it head on and begin taking baby steps by doing things afraid. Move forward and do what you need to do even in the midst of fear. Each time you do, you crush the fearful, anxious spirit and build up the confident spirit within you.

7.) KNOWLEDGE IS POWER - Get informed and find out what you can about the symptoms and causes of panic and anxiety. Many people struggle with anxiety and many have overcome. You are not alone in your struggle and taking a step to inform yourself is a big step to victory.

Getting informed helps equip you with the power to overcome.

Your goal? To start utilizing these tips today. Do not allow anxiety to paralyze your potential. Overcoming is a gradual process, but by applying these tips to your life you can speed up the process. Lift up your head to the light and boldly decide to be all that God created you to be.Now go take steps of personal growth

CHAPTER FIVE

CHALLENGE INTRUSIVE THOUGHTS

DO YOU SUFFER FROM INTRUSIVE THOUGHTS?

It's extraordinary how we humans always tend to think more negatively than positively. Not all of us, but I think it fair to say the majority. If you pay me a nice compliment today, but someone said something negative about me yesterday, although I'd be delighted with what you said about me, I'd gravitate more towards the negative comment.

I'd allow that to take over my thinking, more than the compliment.

Do you suffer from intrusive thoughts? The point is that in almost all cases of General Anxiety Disorder, or G.A.D., the driving factor is anxious thinking. This, then, would be typical. Your compliment, so nice and welcome though it is, would take a back seat to the unpleasant comment, and I'd be far more likely to run this around in my mind, allowing it to fester.

But that's merely one, or rather two, comments.

Thinking in the negative certainly goes back to the days when self-preservation had to be uppermost in our minds. Not necessarily thinking the worst all the time, but always on the lookout for anything that may be dangerous and that could cause us, and members of our tribe, harm.

After all, it isn't the thoughts themselves that cause us so much trouble. It's how we respond to them. Suppose we work in a shop that sells valuable antique china. Naturally enough, we don't want to knock anything over, but the owner's so arranged the merchandise that, unless you're particularly clumsy, you're able to move around the shop in perfect safety.

Most of us would probably be all right. We'd steer well clear of the pieces, but we wouldn't worry ourselves sick over whether or not we'll break any. Unfortunately, the poor person who suffers from G.A.D. won't be quite so lucky. The worry and concern over breaking something will start to consume their life.

Now, thoughts are a form of energy. Basically, they're neither good nor bad. What they need is to be fed by the attention, and to make them 'stick,' they need strong emotional attraction. So the person with General Anxiety Disorder thinks about knocking something over and for a while, the thought just kicks around in their brain.

Then the more attention they give it, the more it likes it, then an emotional reaction sets in and there's the thought of knocking things over, literally being a bull in a china shop, stuck like glue to their mind.

Any type of negative thought may assail you, and it'll do so most forcefully when you're not engaged in any form of activity. The worst thing you can do is to attempt to suppress the thought. The more you try to do so, the more the thought attempts to 'stick.'

After all, it's receiving attention, isn't it, and that's just what it likes.

WHAT ARE INTRUSIVE THOUGHTS?

Have you ever had thoughts that just won't go away?

If you said yes to the question above, then you are experiencing intrusive thoughts. Intrusive thoughts are those thoughts that just won't go away, they are constantly in your head and no matter what you do they just follow you around like a black cloud.

I'm sure this sounds familiar to many people, everyone has these types of thoughts at one point or another in their life, usually when they are worried or stressed about something in their lives. This is completely normal, however, these continuous, unwanted thoughts can become overbearing and start to interrupt your life.

For example, you may have thoughts that bad things are always going to happen and this is constantly in your mind, running over and over again. These thoughts also tend to revolve around health, loved ones or irrational fears.

Intrusive thoughts can occur at any time of the day and if you have them regularly, you may notice them showing up all the time and at the most unwanted time. You can be going about your day, maybe hanging out with friends or family when all the sudden you get these unwanted thoughts and your mind is just stuck on them like the needle on an old record player.

Would you be surprised to hear that intrusive thoughts are part of anxiety disorder?

They definitely are part of anxiety disorder. Anxiety affects people in different ways and intrusive thoughts are just one of them. The good news is that there are cures available for anxiety and these ongoing thoughts.

Intrusive thoughts are often dealt with by people who suffer from Obsessive Compulsive Disorder.

There are many that have dealt with this and felt like they were losing their minds because of it. People in this position often seek out information in regard to it naturally. The problem people in this position find is that sources such as books don't contain the best of information. The writers of books on subjects such as this oftentimes have not gone through it themselves which naturally limits them in their knowledge of the subject. It's unfortunate, but because of the lack of experience on the part of the writers, people who need help will oftentimes seek help from less than worthy sources.

People who suffer from intrusive thoughts, unfortunately, find that oftentimes the methods they use to help themselves are flawed and don't really do enough. People in this position may find that what they are dealing with is actually Obsessive Compulsive Disorder which has been studied quite a bit and has valid solutions. If you are trying to be cured and are doing everything properly and it's not working, that could mean that you are being misinformed. The reason many fail to cure themselves is due to being misinformed.

Dealing with things such as intrusive thoughts can really mess with a person's head. What you want to keep in mind is that you have control over how you handle your situation and that there are things you can do. Many in this position would naturally want a quick fix. Don't rely on quick fixes for things such as this though because they are unreliable and will likely only be temporary if they work at all. The road to healing requires a lot of effort and quite a bit of patience. You need to retrain your brain to handle things differently. It can be done and you can be the one to do it if you are willing to take your time and handle it properly.

You may be seeking out professional help from sources such as counselors or therapists in regard to intrusive thoughts. Seeking professional help is not a bad idea but you don't want to overdo it. There are those out there that attempt to seek help from multiple counselors or therapists. Using multiple therapists or counselors is not a good idea. If anything it could simply confuse you, receiving different advice from different sources.

Utilizing books to help you understand or to treat your intrusive thoughts is not a bad idea. What you must be aware of however is that books are oftentimes written by those who lack the actual experience of dealing with what you are dealing with. Because of lack of experience, they are naturally limited in their understanding of it. Many people out there have attempted to cure themselves and have failed but if that occurs it's very likely that they were misinformed in regard to their treatment. Getting cured of this condition isn't an overnight thing and requires patience. When seeking out professional help stick to using a single source so that you don't become confused. Being confused will only complicate the healing process, which isn't beneficial to you.

INTRUSIVE THOUGHTS AND OBSESSIVE COMPULSIVE DISORDER

The human mind is a complex web of thoughts, emotions, and feelings. The interplay between the three determines an individual's personality. While people do have control over what they think or feel, sometimes, it could be the other way around. Intrusive thoughts creep in without a warning such as those explicitly related to violence and sex and dominate rational thinking. For example, while waiting for the subway train, one may fleetingly consider chucking oneself or a bystander under the rails. Fortunately, thoughts such as these are momentary at best. Soon one gets absorbed in the day-to-day activities and all is forgotten. However, intrusive thoughts have a direct bearing on the development of the obsessive-compulsive disorder (OCD).

While most people do not brood over such ill thoughts for long, those who do may become victims of OCD. For instance, in case of some new mothers who are trying to cope with experiences of motherhood for the first time, the baby could be a cause of distress, and thoughts of beating the baby may emerge in the subconscious. However, when she starts ruminating about the bad thoughts again and again and consciously berates herself for being a dreadful mother, it could be an instance of OCD.

OCD is first manifested as an obsession thereafter, to counter the intrusive thought, there is the act of compulsion or the "undoing." This could also be likened to the act seeking atonement for guilt. During the act of atonement, the mother could repeatedly assure herself that her love for the child is boundless and that she would never harm her child again.

Causes of OCD

Though the exact causes of OCD are unknown, the following factors can increase the risk of OCD:

- **Genes:** Individuals with a family history of OCD are more likely to develop the disorder.

- **Environment:** Past traumatic experiences may contribute to the development of OCD.

- **Brain structure and functioning.** Scientific evidence has revealed that there are differences in the frontal cortex and the subcortical structures of patients with OCD.

> This may determine their response to circumstances and people around them.

Bad thoughts do not make someone a bad person. Explaining the phenomena of intrusive thoughts and its association with anxiety disorder such as OCD, Steve Phillipson, a psychologist specializing in OCD and clinical director for the Center for Cognitive Behavioral Psychotherapy in Midtown Manhattan, says, "First is the idea that the thought, in and of itself, is deviant and signifies something horrible about the person who has it. "I must be a sick, mentally unstable person to have had this thought occur." However, a person who is distressed by such thoughts experiences not only psychological turmoil but also certain physical symptoms such as heart palpitations, rapid breathing, profuse sweating, and confused thinking. Over time, this condition could completely incapacitate the person.

Dealing with intrusive thoughts

It is best not to pay much attention to negative thoughts. However, when such thoughts start to impinge on day-to-day activities, it is best to seek a therapist. One may also consider the following as a means for mastering intrusive thoughts:

- Practicing mindfulness or other forms of mind-relaxing activities

- Reminding oneself that having an intrusive thought does not necessarily translate into the act of doing it.

- Continue doing whatever one was engaged in before the intrusive thought came in

- Practicing deep breathing to ease the anxiety

- Engaging the help of a support group or people living with similar problems.

- Maintaining a journal and recording experiences for cathartic effect.

Road to recovery

One of the most effective means for treating OCD is exposure and response prevention or ERP Therapy. ERP therapy is primarily a subset of cognitive behavioral therapy. As the name implies, this therapy involves patients conjuring images of intrusive thoughts and exposure exercises to help prove that thoughts are not dangerous. An individual with troubling thoughts of attacking someone with a knife could be therapeutically encouraged to leave knives on the table when guests are due, in spite of the graphic intrusive images he/she may have of doing something wrong. To improve treatment outcomes, one must consider the help of a mental health expert at the right time in order to lead a happier life.

PANIC DISORDER AND INTRUSIVE THOUGHTS

Panic and anxiety disorders take many forms, from phobias to social disorders, they are all somehow linked, but without one discernible cause. Traumatic situations, overbearing or absent parents, childhood trauma, reactions to medication, drug abuse, and illness are just some of the potential causes.

The human mind is a complex thing. Those who suffer from panic attacks quite commonly suffer from other mental health issues, such as obsessive-compulsive disorder, or alcohol abuse.

Those who suffer from panic disorder frequently also struggle with intrusive thoughts. Intrusive thoughts are any thoughts that we haven't initiated through our own choice - they pop into our head like an unwanted visitor. Where they become particularly troubling is when the same thoughts continually return, causing us to dwell on them constantly, time and time again. They begin to dominate our lives, to the point that it is hard to concentrate on anything else.

This style of thoughts are sometimes irrational, but can also be rooted in typical worries such as money and personal performance. A panic attack sufferer's intrusive thought could be a constant fear that a loved one will leave or a constant thought that one should be doing better at work. A sufferer can begin to worry unnecessarily about their health, constantly having thoughts that they have an inexplicable disease.

Just as troubling is when a person begins to continually have intrusive or bothersome thoughts about something that seems really innocuous or ridiculous. The sufferer can then begin to worry that they are losing their sanity - they wonder why they can't stop thinking these mad thoughts.

Intrusive thoughts can exacerbate symptoms of prolonged panic disorder. There are few treatments available specifically for these thoughts, and advice is rather rudimentary. If the patient is able to recognize why the intrusive thought keeps returning, then perhaps it is a good first step to understanding the reasoning behind their panic disorder.

If the thought seems to be linked to the panic attack triggers, then it should be discussed with a friend or counselor. If the recurring thoughts are clearly just the sufferer's mind playing tricks on them, a mind running along at 100 mph, then the best defense is a distraction. When the recurring thought returns it may be best to find something else to occupy the mind. This way the 'crazy' thought does not get much 'air-play', and will eventually recede.

Exercise is perhaps the best form of distraction for the panic attack sufferer from these thoughts, as endorphins are also released while one is distracting the mind.

HOW TO ELIMINATE INTRUSIVE THOUGHTS

In almost all cases of general anxiety, the driving factor fuelling the sensations is anxious thinking. Without addressing these intrusive thoughts, there can be little success in eliminating the root of the anxiety.

People who experience anxiety and panic attacks frequently have to deal with the negative side-effects of unwanted thoughts that creep into their minds. These thoughts can range from worries about health, concern over loved ones, or even fears that do not make any rational sense at all but continue to linger in the mind.

Sometimes, the unwanted intrusive thoughts come from previous experiences; other times they are simply bizarre, leaving the person worried as to why such strange thoughts are occurring. In all these cases, the person is upset by anxious thoughts because they are causing distress and worry. I will guide you through a simple two-step process that is in part related to the One Move which I teach but tailored specifically to dealing with anxious thinking.

Anxious Intrusive ThoughtsTackling anxious intrusive thinking effectively requires a two-pronged approach. To eliminate the negative thinking patterns, there needs to be a shift in attitude along with specific visualization tools.

The Attitude Shift It is not the intrusive thoughts in themselves that cause you distress. It is how you are responding to those thoughts. It is the reaction you are having to the thoughts that enables them to have influence and power over you. In order to better understand how unwanted thoughts come about, it helps to paint a playful visual picture of how this happens. This is a fictional example and will help you better understand how to deal with the issue.

Imagine yourself standing on a street and all around you thoughts are floating lazily by. Some of the thoughts are your own, other thoughts are from outside sources you access such as newspapers, TV, magazines, etc. You notice that when you pay attention to a thought it gravitates nearer. The thoughts you ignore float on by.

When you focus and examine a thought up closely, you notice how it connects to another similar thought, and you find yourself jumping from one thought to the next. Sometimes these are practical, day-to-day thoughts such as bills, chores, etc., or the thoughts can be themed by the past or a fantasy/daydream.

In our imagined scenario, you unexpectedly notice a thought hovering in front of you that scares you. This thought is called "Fear X." X could be panic attacks, ill health, or something bizarre. You find it impossible not to look at the thought, and as you give it your full attention, this causes it to come closer and closer. When you examine the thought, you begin to react with fear as you do not like what you see. You further notice how that initial scary thought is connected to more worrying "what if" thoughts that you also examine in detail. The more you try to escape from the thought by pushing it away, the more it seems to follow you around as if it were stuck to you. You try to focus on more pleasant thoughts, but you find yourself continuously coming back to the fearful thought.

Intrusive Thoughts...

There is an expression of "thoughts sticking like glue." The very act of reacting emotionally to the thought glues the thought all the more to you, and the more time you spend worrying and obsessing about the thought, the more that glue becomes hardened over time. The thought and all its associated connected thoughts are there in the morning when you wake and there at night when you are trying to get some sleep. The thought becomes stuck to your psyche because your emotional reaction to it is its sticking power. Thoughts are a form of energy, neither good nor bad. It is how we judge those thoughts that determine how much impact they have on our lives. Thoughts need firstly to be fed by the attention, but what they really love is a good strong emotional reaction to make them stick!

Thoughts that stay with us are first attracted to us by the attention we pay them and then stuck firmly in place by the level of emotional reaction we have to them.

This is an important point. A thought-even negative intrusive thoughts-can only have an influence over you if you allow it to. The emotional reaction from us is a thought's energy source. What's interesting is that either a positive or a negative emotional reaction is fine for the thought. Energy and attention are what it is attracted to. Once you are having an emotional reaction to a thought, you will be regularly drawn to that thought until the emotional reaction has lost its energy and faded away.

For example, if someone you know pays you a very positive compliment, you may find yourself unintentionally drawn to that thought anytime you have a spare moment. You probably find it improves your overall level of confidence and mood throughout the day. Sadly, however, we tend to focus less on the positive and more on the negative. We seem to forget those positive compliments all too easily and are drawn more frequently to what might upset us. Taking the opposite example, if someone you know insults you, I am sure that you find the emotional reaction to that thought much more intense and probably very long-lasting.

So the basic pattern of thinking is as follows:

If you are not engaged with an activity or task, your mind will tend to wander to any thoughts that you are having a strong emotional reaction to. In general, as they are the ones that you are probably reacting most strongly to, angry or fearful thoughts seem to surface quickly.

What I am suggesting is that the most ineffective way to eliminate intrusive thoughts is not to try and suppress them. Thought suppression studies, (Wegner, Schneider, Carter, & White, 1987) have proven that the very act of trying to suppress a thought, only results in a higher frequency of unwanted intrusive thoughts occurring. This recurrence of the thought has been termed the 'rebound effect'. Simply put: the more you try suppressing a thought, the more the unwanted thought keeps popping up (rebounding).

So how do we begin to tackle this problem of intrusive thoughts?

There needs to be a change of attitude. By a change in attitude, I mean a change in the way you have been reacting to the intrusive thoughts. A change in attitude will quickly disarm the emotional reaction you are having to the fearful thoughts. Once the emotional reaction has been significantly reduced, the anxious intrusive thoughts will dissipate. In the past, you have probably tried to rid yourself of the thoughts by attempting to struggle free of them.

The trick, however, is not to attempt to be free of them but to have a new reaction to them when they run through your mind. We can never fully control what goes through our minds, but we can control how we react to what goes on there. That is the key difference between someone who gets caught up in fearful thinking and someone who does not.

The thoughts that terrify us are not fuelled by some unknown force; they are our own. We empower them and equally we dismiss them. When you have an uncomfortable thought you would rather not be thinking, your first reaction is usually to tense up internally and say to yourself, "Oh no, I don't like that idea. I don't want that thought right now." The very act of trying to push these intrusive thoughts away and then understandably getting upset when that does not work causes the thoughts to become more stuck to your psyche.

It's like saying to your mind over and over again

"whatever you do, do not think of pink elephants," and guess what? You can't get a single thought in that is not related to pink elephants.

As long as you struggle with the thought, your mind, like a bold child, will keep returning to it. This is not to say your mind is maliciously working against you. It is better to compare the mind to a radar scanner that picks up on thoughts within us that have high levels of emotional reaction connected to them.

To not react emotionally to intrusive thoughts you need to learn to disempower the "fear factor" of the thought; then you must accept and be comfortable with whatever comes to mind. Don't hide from or push the anxious thoughts away.

So to take an example:

Say you have fear "X" going on in your mind. That fear can be virtually anything your mind can conceive. You know the thoughts are not a realistic fear, and you want them to stop interrupting your life.

Next time the fearful thought comes to mind, do not push it away. This is important.

Tell yourself that that is fine and that the thought can continue to play in your mind if it wishes, but you are not going to give it much notice and you are certainly not going to qualify it by reacting with fear. You know in your heart that the thought is very unlikely to happen. You have a deeper sense of trust and will not be tossed around emotionally all day by a thought. Say to yourself:

"Well that thought/fear is a possibility, but it is very remote and I am not going to worry about that right now. Today I am trusting that all is well."

What is of key importance is not to get upset by the thoughts and feelings as they arise. To avoid any fearful emotional reaction to the fear/thought gives the fearsome cartoon characteristics.

Imagine, for example, it is Donald Duck telling you that "Something awful is going to happen. Aren't you scared?" Give the character a squeaky voice and make it a totally ridiculous scene. How can you take seriously an anxious duck with his big feet? This use of cartoon imagery reprograms the initial emotional reaction you might have had to the thought and eliminates any authority the thought may have over you. You are reducing the thought's threat. When that is done, move your attention back to whatever you were doing. Remember, you are not trying to push the thought away or drown it out with some outside stimulus.

This takes practice in the beginning, but what will happen is that you will find yourself checking how you think/feel less and less during the day, and as it does not have a strong fearful emotion connected to it, your mind will not be drawn to troublesome intrusive thoughts. To put in another way, the thought becomes unstuck and fades away because the emotional reaction has been neutralized. In fact, that is the first step to moving away from anxious thoughts--neutrality. It is as if your mental energy was spinning in a negative cycle while you were caught in the anxious intrusive thoughts. Now, you are learning to stop the negative cycle, and move into neutral (see illustration below).

From this new position of neutrality, you will experience a much greater sense of clarity away from the confusion of an overanxious mind. Moving into this mindset of neutrality is your first step. Thoughts generally lead us in one direction or another -a positive cycle (peace/sense of control and order) or a negative cycle (anxiety/ fear/ disorder). The next step is to adopt a relaxed peaceful state of mind and move your energy into a positive cycle of thinking.

You might have wondered why it is that some people seem more susceptible to worries and unwanted intrusive thoughts than others. You now know the answer to that. The difference is that the people who seem carefree are the ones who are not reacting with strong fearful emotion to an anxious thought. These people see the same array of thoughts as an anxious person, but they do not make a fearful thought a part of their lives. They dismiss the thought or laugh it off and have a sense of trust that things will work out fine. They see no point in reacting with fear to these thoughts, and that ensures the thought has no power or authority over them. You may feel that you are by nature an anxious person and that you will always react with fear to these thoughts because you have done so for years. That is not the case. Continuous or obsessive anxious thinking is a behavioral habit, and just like any habit, it can be unlearned. I have outlined the quickest and most effective way to do this by using a unique shift in attitude. You can undo years of anxious thinking and reduce your level of general anxiety very quickly. All it takes is practice.

CHAPTER SIX

HOW CBT CAN TREAT ADOLESCENT DEPRESSION AND SUICIDAL THOUGHTS

USING CBT TO TREAT EMOTIONAL PROBLEMS

Life is tough. It can surprise you with lots of happiness and yet, sometimes the surprises may not be so pleasant. When people are faced with tough situations, their responses can be quite varied. In some cases, people go off the rocker emotionally, when faced with untold grief and sorrow.

Emotional well-being and a healthy sense of optimism are required for normal living. A healthy hope for the future is quite essential, as people need to be able to look forward to something pleasant. However, some people get depressed and need emotional therapy to be nursed back to health. Depression can be extremely dangerous, as it robs people of a zest for living. Life looks all gray and bleak. That is why CBT or Cognitive Behavior Therapy is quite in demand around the globe. Everyone is raving about how CBT is effective in treating depression.

Let's look at how CBT is able to help depressive patients. CBT acts on the basic premise that we live out our lives based on what and how we think. Thoughts give rise to feelings and also impact actions. One of the ways to change moods, feelings, and actions is to change the thoughts that cause them. CBT aims at helping people explore their thoughts so that they can examine these closely. Depression and suicidal tendencies are caused by negative thoughts as well as the caused feelings of despondency. When these thoughts are replaced by positive and optimist thoughts, it becomes possible to dispel the depression and bring about healing.

Patients of depression are required to have extended sessions with CBT experts and therapists. The CBT therapist helps the patient recount his/her experiences. This helps the patient and the therapist to jointly pinpoint the causes of the depression. All negative thoughts are isolated and replaced by positive thoughts. Little by little, the patient is able to see a ray of hope. There is a gradual outbreak of optimism. These are the first signs that the patient is making some progress towards recovery.

CBT needs a lot of patience as well as hard work on the part of the patient as well as the therapist. It is not a quick fix solution. At the same time, the therapist should also be very competent as depressive patients can be quite tough to handle

CHAPTER SEVEN

OPTIMAL LIFE-MANAGEMENT SKILLS AND TIPS TO FOLLOW TO START THIS LIFE-CHANGING ROAD TO SUCCESS AND FULFILLMENT

STRESS MANAGEMENT ESSENTIALS

We do not doubt that the world can be an extremely stressful place. This is precisely why we must implement the best possible stress management techniques to keep these solutions working for us. Given the state of the economy, rising costs, and the level of employment, it's best to do your best, but even when you are very focused upon your job, you should still have the time to enjoy activities which will help you to manage stress and enjoy your life to the fullest. Thank goodness stress management skills are skills that you can apply even if they don't come naturally to you. You can begin to learn these valuable techniques today.

You Might Be Asking: Why Bother With Managing

Stress?

One good reason to learn effective techniques to manage your stress levels is the fact that stress takes a toll on the body, and that there are many hidden ways in which it manifests. Are any of these symptoms visible in your life?

For example, do you ever have digestive problems, difficulty sleeping, depression, anxiety, or regular headaches? If so, these are indications that you will benefit from implementing stress relief techniques into your daily life.

Once you do so, you can expect many beneficial results, such as increased resistance to illness, reduced anxiety, better sleeping habits, lower blood pressure, better happiness, better relationships with others and the list goes on.

Stress Relief Works! So Now You Might Ask, What Can I Do To Obtain This?

There are many resources available for you today to relieve stress. For example, you can try a yoga class, meditation, and implementing laughter therapy into your regular routines. Yes, there is scientific evidence that proves that there are great benefits obtained from the exercise of laughter. Furthermore, studies have shown that consistently paying attention to your levels of stress helps to keep you healthy.

People often underestimate the benefits of laughter and the power of positive thinking. Before you even get out of bed in the morning, your mood is usually set, so why not try setting it in a manner that is more helpful to you? If you start your day with a positive affirmation, then surely you will have an easier time dealing with the rest of the day. Does that "guarantee" a great day? Of course not, but it does give you the best skills and techniques to work with which will, in turn, help you face the challenges you encounter in the best way possible.

Optimism The Healthiest Choice You Can Make!

It might be challenging to change your frame of mind, but it can be done, with consistent practice. Some people are naturally optimistic, so pay attention to how they relate to life as they may have some pointers for you Even if you are naturally pessimistic, you can nevertheless train yourself to see the good in your life and in the things around you if you are willing to make the effort.

Here are some good tips which can help you:

• Notice when you use negative language or speak badly about yourself, then change that habit by nipping it in the bud and making it a positive statement instead.

• Journaling is great exercise! List only good things about yourself and about your day.

• Try not to engage in negative conversations with negative people.

Try these ideas for just 7 days and you will be surprised at how much these tiny changes can have a huge effect upon your mood and upon your stress levels. Successful stress management techniques begin with small steps like these but they end with huge changes in the level of quality in your life.

THE ROAD TO SUCCESS

Success is something everyone desires, but few are willing to pay the price to obtain. Success is a process and the stages of this process are:

- The initial stage

- The progressive stage

- The achievement stage

The initial stage begins with a dream; a desire or goal for something more. It's something that occupies our thoughts and puts excitement in our lives. Children are often like this. They are filled with dreams and believe that they can achieve them until those dreams are dashed by the negativity of those around them and unbelief that "seems" to come with age. Our society is geared toward negativity and if we believe only in what we see and hear, we give up on our dreams and begin to follow the pack. It is no wonder that Jesus said that unless one becomes like a little child, he cannot enter the kingdom of God. Child-like belief is necessary to obtain our dreams and achieve our goals. Dare to be a child again. Dare to dream big dreams and even more; dare to fulfill them! Write your goals down. Read them often until your subconscious mind begins to diligently work on them and come up with ideas or hunches to fulfill them. Remember, the road to success is a road not traveled by the masses.

The majority of people (some 90% or more) are like ships without a rudder. They travel through life aimlessly under the dictates of the blowing winds or their environment and "so-called" luck. Thy has no major goals. They just drift to their graves with little to show for their lives. Most only care for their little world and never realize the unlimited possibilities untapped and waiting to be discovered.

Once a clear major goal is decided, the journey must begin to achieve it. Thus we come to the progressive stage. This is the hard part because the path to success is fraught with "seeming" failure, doubt, and obstacles. Why is this? I believe it is because every person who desires to reach their goals and obtain their dreams must be tested. How bad do you want to reach your goal(s)? What kind of price are you willing to pay? Can you take disappointment? Can you get back up when you are knocked down? All of this will determine your level of success. I also think that the trials along the way only make it sweeter when the destination is reached. The key to this stage is not to give up too soon. Don't be like the gold miner that started to dig for gold and got discouraged and gave up too soon. In his disappointment, he sold his land and equipment to someone else who only had to dig another foot to find the richest vein of gold ever discovered! You never know how far you are from reaching your goal. It only takes one circumstance or person to drastically change everything for the good! One moment of favor outweighs an entire lifetime of labor and you never know when favor will appear in your life.

To get from where you are today to where you want to be you will be faced with giants. The first giant you will face in doubt. The big bully of doubt comes in all forms. He could come as a relative saying, "Are you nuts; that won't work! Why are you wasting your time?" Your spouse may say, "You've tried things like this before and failed; quit wasting our money." Others will say, "That seems too risky, you better be safe rather than sorry."

The next giant you will face is fear (doubt and fear are buddies). You may experience the "allusion" of the fear of loss, the fear of failure and defeat or the fear of rejection and humiliation. These fears come out of nowhere and "appear" very real. But remember, they are only appearances. After all, fear in 90% of the cases is just False Evidence Appearing Real.

All types of things may happen, but do not lose hope. It is imperative that you stay the course because, remember, that you are being tested for the right of passage to your major goal. Once you pass the test, your dream will, without a doubt, become reality.

What an exciting day when you have obtained your goal. You have become successful! What a joy to say that you made it! Think about how Thomas Edison must have felt after over 10,000 seeming "failures" he finally developed the incandescent light bulb that changed the world forever! You too will experience that joy if you just hang in there. Keep your mind set on the things you want and use your will and passion (emotion) to keep your mind focused. Hang on to your dream(s); fight for your goal(s) and before you know it you will reach them, only to begin again to pursue better and bigger dreams, which, by the way, seem easier to obtain after passing down the road to success the first time. You can do it. You can be in the top 10% who live a successful life. Go for it! Make your dreams come true.

LEARNING NEW SKILLS KEEP YOU ON THE ROAD TO SUCCESS

Learning new skills is essential to keep on being successful in your job. If you don't feel fulfilled in your job and you would like to improve your position in the company you are working for then you will probably need to develop more skills so you can get ahead in your career.

If you feel very passionate about moving ahead in your career then you'll need to sit back and think about how well you really perform in your current job. You should take a good look at where you need to improve and better yourself. Start by making a list of the areas in your life you need to work on. Maybe you can talk to the boss or your supervisor about what steps you need to take to improve your skills to ensure that you will have a better chance to be considerate for a better portion.

Reaching the heights of being successful in the company you are working for may not be an easy task. It requires hard work and a very steady focus. You'll really need to educate yourself and do some courses. To make sure you get the most out of what you are learning you would need to pick up special lessons in every endeavor you undertake. This will be very helpful for building up your competence in your chosen industry.

Learning new skills will equip you with new knowledge that will make you more competitive. This will enable you to overcome the new challenges you will be presented with as you conquer new grounds. If you really want to be successful and get ahead in your career then you may want to attend career enhancement seminars such as leadership training and management workshops.

You can find programs specific for any type of career you have chosen as well as personal development. To be on a personal development journey is a very exciting path to be on, it will bring you out of your comfort zone and guide you in the direction of where you were meant to go.

You may want a complete career change or maybe you just want to improve your current situation in your career so you can get the sense of fulfillment you feel is missing in your existing job. You spend many hours in your job so it is important that you are happy there because if you are not happy in your job it will affect your well being as well as your health.

Learning New Skills will help you prepare yourself for all types of challenges and obstacles you may meet in your life. It will also help you become more focused on achieving your goals and objectives so that you can become more successful in life. You will feel more contented, more fulfilled and more satisfied with yourself and this will certainly increase your confidence and self-esteem. The benefits you will gain by learning new skills are countless.

HOW TO BECOME SUCCESSFUL AND LIVE THE LIFE THAT YOU ALWAYS WANTED

Are you currently living the life that you always wanted? Or, do you want more out of life than the regular "going to bed-going to work-going home-going to bed" routine every single day? Well, this chapter is intended for those who want some excitement in their lives and at the same time, want to ditch the boring do-the-same old thing day after day after day.

1. Write Down Your Goals

All of us have goals that we want to reach. Whether it's going to school; losing weight; learning to play an instrument; learning how to cook; learning a new language; starting a business; writing a book; travel around the world; etc. What you need to do is brainstorm about what you want to do and write them down on a paper (you write them down in your phone as well.) Once you have written them down, put it something where you can see it, such as your desk, dresser, near a mirror, on a wall, etc. This is important because it gives you a reminder every single day on what you really want to do in your life.

2. Write Down Your Plans

It is very important to have goals that you want to accomplish and dreams of a better life. Once you have written those goals and dreams down, you must come up with a timetable in order to figure out what type of action you need to take to reach them. Determine and write down the short-term and long-term action you need to take for each dream and goal and figure out how to execute the plan. You see, a plan without execution equals a waste of time and energy on your account. By having a plan with the right execution, it creates a point of no return where it's too late to turn back now and you must forge ahead with your plans.

3. Motivation

Ah, yes! This is the point where we see the private lives of an athlete or a celebrity on television or in the magazine (with the cars, house, the fame, etc.); or you see that someone created a business and after a while it becomes successful. Then, you compare your current life to the celebrity in question and you say to yourself "I want to have a lifestyle just like that." IT CAN HAPPEN- Nothing is impossible! But, it is up to you to make some changes in your life to create that magic. The idea of having a better life than the one that you're currently living right now should be one of the best motivation tactics out there. If that isn't enough, think about the people who either laughed at you or thought you were crazy when you told them about your plans. Who are these people? These folks (a.k.a.- the non-believers, the naysayers, the haters) think that you are wasting your time with your dreams and goals (they refer them as a pipe dream) and might actually tell you to give up.

A bit of advice: DON'T EVER GIVE UP! All you have to do is work hard every single day to accomplish your dreams and goals--and make sure that the plans you created going through without stopping. Then, you have been successful in reaching the desired goal, you can tell those non-believers, naysayers and haters where they can go!

4. Don't Procrastinate

All of us are guilty of this. If we have to do something, we'll say "Oh, I'll get it tomorrow." Well, tomorrow comes and nothing happens. Then we'll push it off until the next day, then the next week, then the next month. Once the year ends, you look back and say to yourself "I should have done this...." Procrastination is the #1 killer of being successful. Don't put anything off that you can do today. Get started right now and never let the phrase "I'll get to it tomorrow" creep into your mind. Do it now!

5. Persistence

The road in becoming successful is not a smooth one. You will experience some ups and downs. There will some days where everything is clicking and other times where nothing goes right.

The message here is this: Never Give Up! Here are two examples of what persistence can help and actually motivate you in reaching your goals:

NBA legend Michael Jordan was cut from his high school team in 10th grade. Did he let that set back stop him? No! Actually, he used that failure as motivation during his playing days in the National Basketball Association to win 6 championships and 6 MVP Awards. In a classic Nike commercial, he openly admits to the many times he tried and failed in winning basketball games when he was a player. Go to YouTube and watch his Nike commercials about accepting failure and use that fuel the fire of success.

Another example is Thomas Edison, one of the greatest inventors in history. Edison tried and failed 10,000 times in reshaping the light bulb. Did he think about giving up after trying time and time again? No! Edison, in a famous quote about failure, said: I have not failed. I have found 9,999 ways that do not work." Edison believed that failure was a mere stepping stone to the road to success.

6. Associate with successful people

It's like the old saying "Birds Of A Feather Flock Together" along with the old adage " You will act just like the people you'll associate with." If you hang around with successful people, after a while, there's a good chance that their success could rub off on you. Likewise, if you hang around those who are involved in crime and other shady things--then they are going to lead you to a path of destruction.

If you want to become successful, find out and connect with those individuals who have made it and pick their brain on what does it take to reach that level of success. Go to different business functions and self-help seminars and network with as many people as you can. The goal here is to network and develop contacts.

7. Passion

If you don't have any passion for something that you want to do, you better find it quickly! You see, passion is required in having the life that you always wanted. You must have that fire and desire to put all that energy into something reaching your goals. You must enjoy what you are doing because you would rather spend the majority of your time doing something that you love.

So, what if you can't find your passion? Well, there are some ways that you can find it:

A. Brainstorm- Find a quiet place and think about what you always wanted to do. It doesn't matter what it is. Remember, this is your life and you make all the decisions, not anyone else.

B. Don't quit your job- If you do have a job, don't quit just yet. If your goals are to start a business, wait until the venture has started making a steady income. You don't want to be that person who quit their day job to start a business and the venture becomes a financial bust and you end up being broke without employment.

C. Research- Go to the library, online or a bookstore and do some research. Send an email to the corporation or a specific individual and find out how they were able to get started. Use their information like the blueprint to your success. Buy some self-discovery or self-help books or read some magazine about people who were able to persevere through their obstacles in life and become successful. Use their inspirational stories and go on from there.

D. Don't Quit- You will never know when a great opportunity comes around if you decide to pack it and give up. We always hear the "I should have done this" saying in our heads every time we look back in our lives. Keep pursuing your dreams and goals until you will become successful.

8. Optimistic

In order to reach a successful life, you are going to find out that everything will not go your way all of the time. For every perfect attempt at something, there will be hundreds, maybe thousands of times where it doesn't go well and you say to yourself" I give up," "I quit," "I will never get this done right," or "I suck."

Hey, you must always look at the bright side when you are making an attempt to reach your desired goal(s). Nothing will go as plan. You must have a positive attitude in everything you do. Also, it is very important to have the confidence and believe that you will reach your goal(s) one day. Every day, you must say to yourself " I am going to give it my all in everything I do. I believe in myself and I will reach my goals no matter how long it will take."

OVERCOME FAILURE

Success in life is known to be tied with the extraordinary. Being successful takes work, lots of work. These type of people who succeed in life are those who study hard and then play hard later. These type of people are those who are never satisfied with "okay" or "fine" or being average because these people want to be something other than the ordinary. Are you willing to stand out of the crowd? Do you want to drive to be the absolute best, along with exceeding your mental capacity and means?

Of course, you do. The real question here is if you carry that ability and desire. Whether you do or don't, the road to success has already started, and you're late to the game if you haven't begun yet.

The number one rule of success is that you must go beyond to what you're used to. This means that you will do more work than what is presented in order to achieve greatness. Anyone who is a successful being is aware of this. They are the overachiever. Instead of accepting a job well done when it is fulfilled, they do more than that; they go out of their ways until the job is considered an amazing job; a pat on the back. These people are someone you would consider that goes beyond their work.

There is no secret to where this kind of work ethic can be shown. Whether it is in school or at work, success is everywhere-success transfers through part of life. It doesn't matter where one demonstrates success because it is automatically shown where ever they go. It is like a laser beam that shines through, which is unavoidable as success takes one as far as they can imagine.

The next so-called 'secret' of success is having persistence. Fell down? Then get back up and get back on the road! For every time when you don't get back up, someone will take that spot and claim it for themselves-not being you fell down at the wrong time, but because you put it off for someone else to take due to your procrastination.

By being persistent, it means that one is willing to do the work over and over until it is finished until it is accomplished. When you know what you want in life and are willing to do what it takes, you are on the right road to success. Many individuals end their journey here because the work either becomes too tough, too repetitive, or just a whole bunch of excuses that is imaginable made up. But remember that by having persistence, you stay in the game, and you continue to be in the game until greatness comes.

Ready to change your mindset? Good, because you will need the mindset of not saying "this is too much" but rather "this will be accomplished". Start believing that nothing is too much because as previously mentioned, success will take one far.

Your ability to overcome errands on top of errands means that you are able to handle whatever is thrown at you. You aren't willing to stop until it is all finished with. Even if it means years of work to finish. This is a must because every successful individual knows that life is full of surprises along with non-stop journeys. When something hits you hard, you find a way to take it down-you overcome any obstacle that stands in your way.

By being successful, you also need to work smart.

Working smart means you're able to apply your ability to the right opportunity for success. Not only does success include going beyond, being persistent, believing that nothing is too much, and working smart, it also requires you to take advantage of opportunities that luckily come across. That way, you aren't wasting your time when you put in work that eventually leads to nowhere. That's what working smart means. It is your mind foreseeing what can best be applied to any scenario.

Flaming enthusiasm, backed up by horse sense and persistence, is the quality that most frequently makes for success. - Dale Carnegie

Everything that has been said about succeeding sounds all too much to retain doesn't it?

That's because it is, and for your benefits, you will need to develop an ambitious attitude because successful people are ambitious from the start to the end. These are the same folks that stayed up late during school nights, reading from textbooks to understand algorithms, physic equations, and whatnot. They didn't do it because they were cramming for the exam that was to be taken the following morning, wrong! They did it because their curiosity spiked upon their imagination, and they wanted to understand why or how it came to be.

The trait of being ambitious is a must. In order to

succeed, there must be a strong desire of wanting success. When there is something that doesn't go your way, you will redo it over and over you reach to get it your way, and that's all due to the intention that your ambition holds. Without ambition means that you have no strong desire to want.

Success is to be measured not so much by the position that one has reached in life as by the obstacles which he has overcome. - Booker T. Washington

If you were to be trapped underneath the water and you wanted to take that breath so badly, but you couldn't, what would be the first thing on your mind? Would it be your plans for the weekend? Of course not! (or at least I hope not!) That would be the last thing you would want to think about because here you are, struggling hopelessly for a breath of air. The only thing you want is to breathe, and that defines ambition.

Successful people know it is never enough. Successful people are motivated, have goals, and go beyond than the average Joe. They have something inside them that drives their passion, vision, and focus. It's their ability to keep on going even when everything in life tries so hard to stop them. Accomplishing those goals is what sets them apart while defining the meaning of success. Whether you have what it takes, the road to success has already started, and you're late to the game if you haven't begun.

What is a success? I think it is a mixture of having a flair for the thing that you are doing; knowing that it is not enough, that you have got to have hard work and a certain sense of purpose. - Margaret Thatcher

CHAPTER EIGHT

BREAK BAD HABITS AND ENJOY LIFE

BAD HABITS

What are bad habits?

According to a study from the Massachusetts Institute of Technology, habit-forming activities alter a specific region of the brain known as the basal ganglia, an area vital to habits and addictions. Part of this change resembles that of taking on a memory of the habit. With this memory, a habit can be triggered if again exposed to the old cues, making it difficult to break bad habits.

A habit is an urge to carry out an action or behavior no matter the consequences. There are healthy habits and unhealthy habits. But the ones that seem to destroy us are the unhealthy ones. Bad habits get in the way of our goals and the ability to achieve them. They have the capability to dominate your life, forming a shackle around you, and making a slave out of you. Before realizing it, your negative habit will become your master and everything you do will revolve around it. You will lie, cheat or deceive just to maintain your habit. You will become a puppet to your bad habit. You can have the toughest of characters, it doesn't matter - the negative habits will restrain you from making the progress you are truly capable of in your life. It will own you!

Bad habits don't appear bad at first encounter. The first greasy burger, the first inhale from smoking pot, the first snort of cocaine, the first cigarette, the first drink, the first time you cheated on your mate, the first gambling session, the first lie, or the first time you yelled at the kids. The first time you still feel in control. Even the second time is not so bad. But the compulsion quickly takes over, especially if the stimulus has highly addictive qualities. When this happens, even though the mind may want to say "no", the body's addiction holds you hostage to the habit.

We all would like to think we are in control of our own lives. You tell yourself "nothing can ever control me." You spend an enormous amount of time and money to ensure that so many aspects of your life are intact but there is that one little secret of that bad habit that is slowly undermining you and the credibility to seek to maintain.

Use the information to bring honest introspection to your life. If you see someone running down the highway into oncoming traffic, would you run after them to save them? Of course, you will! So it is with a bad habit. Wouldn't you want to save yourself from a bad habit that can potentially destroy you and prevent you from achieving your optimum?

Identifying Unhealthy Habits

The first step in breaking bad habits is to identify them. I mentioned certain specific habits above but negative habits can also come in other forms. For example, you may have a habit of criticizing others or gossiping. You may be a constant worrier suffering from severe anxiety and insomnia. You may be a compulsive shopper and financially irresponsible. Whatever the habit, you must first seek to identify it.

There are times when it can be difficult to identify our bad habits. As human beings, we tend to associate with people who enable our habits. By doing so, the guilt and shame of the habit are disguised. Before long, the unhealthy habit begins to define you. You become known as the sex addict, or the television junkie, or the obese one. Look at yourself in the mirror and be honest with yourself. Identifying your bad habits is a form of acceptance of your habit, which is the first step toward kicking it.

So can you identify your unhealthy habits? Many of you are already aware of what they are. When I had had a problem with substance abuse the following were things I asked myself:

- Is (fill in this space with the bad habit) holding me back from achieving my goal(s)?

- Does (fill in this space with the bad habit) make me feel good about myself?

- Is (fill in this space with the bad habit) something I feel proud of?

- Is (fill in this space with the bad habit) something I feel comfortable doing in the open around my friends and family without causing me embarrassment?

- Is (fill in this space with the bad habit) something I would encourage my child to do?

- Do I listen to the advice of loved ones when they identify my negative habits or do I get on the defensive?

Begin today to identify your bad habits. If you are having difficulty, find a life coach who can help you. Once your negative habits are identified, your coach will assist you in kicking the habit or help you find a professional who can. Before long you will be able to take back your life and accomplish all the goals you have set for you.

Examine Your Bad Habits

Once you have identified your bad habits, it's time to

examine them to see how they affect your life. There are certain things to look for when examining these habits.

1. Examine how much time and effort goes into this habit. This helps you to bring into your conscious mind the extent of your habit. Think about how many years you have been stuck in this habit. Start to monitor your time by keeping a daily log of how much time you are engaged in this habit. For example, if your habit is to sit and watch TV for hours, add up the number of hours spent in front of the TV. Add it all up - the number of hours per day, per month, per year, times the number of years. Use this knowledge to become aware of how much of your precious time is wasted and how much control the television has over your life.

2. Examine how much money is spent on your habit. Make a conscious effort to log the amount of money you spend daily on your habit. For example, if your habit is drinking alcohol, add up how much you spend at the bars, or at the liquor store on a daily basis. Add it up at the end of the week and multiply it by the number of months or years you are stuck in this habit. Become aware of how your hard earned dollar is wasted by your bad habit.

3. Examine your motive for indulging in your habit. For example, if your habit is drinking, look inside to see what it is you are trying to numb. Is it a bad

relationship, or a painful childhood, or some type of emotional trauma? If you cannot identify the motive, you must seek professional guidance to get to the core of your habit and resolve it.

4. Examine the effects of your habit. How is it hurting your health, your spouse, your family, or your relationships? Are you putting your job in jeopardy? Is your bad habit causing you to put off doing important things in your life? Is it affecting your ability to think clearly? Is it getting in the way of achieving your goals?

Once you have taken an inventory of your negative habit, sit and process the following information.

- Do I want to continue down the same path?

- Am I willing to allow this habit to exert that much control over my life?

- Am I willing to let another day go by stranded in my delinquent habit?

- Do I see a need for change in my life?

Changing Your Negative Habits

Depending on the habit, you may need the help of a professional. Habits such as substance abuse, alcoholism, obesity, or gambling will require assistance. There are also many bad habits that you can change on your own. Whatever the habit, you must first make the decision for change. You must accept the fact that you have a problem habit and see the need for change.

The key to breaking negative habits is to disrupt the brain's pattern of doing things. When engaged in a habit the brain becomes locked into a routine that allows the habit to become "second nature" so to speak. This disruption begins the mental preparation that is a necessary part of breaking your habit. You will be able to draw your motivation and determination to break the habit when the mind is set and ready for change. One the change occurs in the mind, the physical behavior follows.

Most of us don't enjoy feeling controlled by anyone or anything. See your bad habit as a form of control and prepare yourself to take back control of your life. This will give you the self-discipline and self-control you need to stay clear of your bad habit.

HOW TO REPLACE BAD HABITS

Habits are one of the hardest things to break or get rid of, and yet, if you know how to replace bad habits with good ones, you can mold and create a better you which give you better opportunities in business and life. It may somehow look complicated but is not an impossible feat to achieve.

So what does it take to make the switch?

You should know that habits are part of your unconscious mind which gives an automatic order to your brain to react, in spite of whatever situation or the moment you are in. A good example of this is checking your phone, even when you are not waiting for any call or message.

Habits, good or bad, are created by doing or practicing something every day until it becomes a wholly natural thing to do, such as driving a car, riding a bicycle or using a phone.

Such behaviors do not only become second nature after a while but can also turn into an obsession, and that is even worse to get rid of but again, not impossible to do. It requires a lot of self-control and discipline on your part. No one else, you and only you can take care of this matter.

But what causes bad habits in the first place? Well, among the many, there are two primary reasons for this.

The Two Primary Reasons

Bad habits usually come down from two major reasons such as being stressed and bored.

Everything you do, such as checking your phone all

the time to partying every weekend to maxing your credit cards to spending hours on social media, could be a response to stress and boredom.

You should know that there is always a possibility to teach yourself new tricks and healthier ways which you can then put into place, this way substituting your unhealthy habits.

But you should also realize that sometimes these odd habits may be the cause of deeply rooted problems. These issues can often be unpleasant to think about, but if you are serious about making changes and replace harmful behaviors, then you have, to be honest with yourself.

Ask yourself why you have such unfavorable habits? What are the reasons for such actions? Is it something that happened to you? Maybe some circumstances, fear, an incident, or even a belief that is now causing you to hold on to a thing that isn't good for you?

You have to identify which causes created your bad habits in the first place because it is crucial to defeating them.

What Do Bad Habits Do

If you have habits right now, good or bad, they are in your life for a reason you generated. It is like staying in a relationship that is not okay for you, smoking or using drugs. In many instances, your bad habits are a simple approach to coping with situations or events that arise in your life.

Once, I stayed for nine years in a relationship in which I gave it my all but where my partner rarely did do a thing, all of this in the hope that she would change at some point in our bond. But it never did happen!

It may be that by checking your phone or social media every five minutes, it might make you feel connected somehow. But you should know that at the same time such behavior often destroys your productivity, divides your attention span, and overpowers you with unwanted stress.

Maybe, it prevents you from feeling like you are "missing out" on something, and so you do it again and again.

Not Possible to Simply Eradicate

As you already know, your negative habits provide you with some relief in your life, and it is very challenging just to eradicate them. Instead, you have to replace your bad habits with good ones who would provide a relaxed feeling but in a positive way.

In other words, your unhealthy habits state certain needs in your life. So, it is better to learn how to replace your bad habit with a healthier and actual behavior that attends that same need.

You cannot expect to simply get rid of a bad habit without even thinking of replacing them. If you try to do so, some of your wants won't be met, and it would be hard to make any new habit stick to become a routine, and so, you will go back to your old ways of doing.

5 SIMPLE STEPS FOR CHANGING A HABIT

"Good habits are hard to develop but easy to live with" and "Bad habits are easy to develop but hard to live with", according to Brian Tracey, a well-known motivational teacher. You may recognize that to successfully manage habit changes, breaking bad habits may be required in order to develop new ones.

Breaking bad habits takes at least 21 days. Of course, in difficult cases, it can take as long as a year. Here's an example of the process of how to change an unhealthy habit to a healthy habit. Suppose you've decided that coffee is not good for you and right now, you drink coffee with sugar daily. The new habit you would like to institute is to drink herbal tea without sugar.

At first, it may be challenging to break the bad habit of drinking coffee. You will have to use self-discipline for the first few weeks but gradually it will get easier. Once you are able to change the old habit to a new healthier one, it will serve you very well. Habits are remarkable because they don't require thinking. You just "do it" for years until you find yourself changing the habit again.

Here are 5 easy steps for changing habits:

1. Awareness: You must become aware of your habits. What is this habit exactly? How is this bad habit or group of bad habits affecting you? How is this habit affecting others? For example, smoking often has negative effects on others as well as on you.

2. Wanting to Change: As someone with a health problem, you must decide that breaking bad habits through a conscious effort is a worthy goal. You must convince yourself that the change in the habit is worth the effort involved.

3. Commitment: You must be determined to do whatever it takes for breaking bad habits so that you can better control your life. You make a decision that "no matter what" you will change the habit. You do the work required to stop. Here are some examples of habits you might want to change: Smoking, eating too much, eating processed foods, not exercising, drinking coffee or other beverages with caffeine in them, eating too much sugar or fat, drinking alcohol, procrastinating, etc.

4. Consistent Action: It is important to focus on changing just one habit at a time. Then, take consistent daily actions for breaking the bad habit that has been causing problems and take the actions to develop a new one. We suggest doing this process one step at a time rather than trying to do it all at once. Sometimes changing a habit can be done "cold turkey" like smoking and sometimes it works better to make a gradual change.

Be sure to give yourself positive rewards often for taking small actions toward changing a bad habit. Continual day-by-day actions are what are critical. This is NOT about an occasional action or step. It is about being consistent every day.

5. Perseverance: There will be times when you question whether it is all worth it. You'll say to yourself that breaking these bad habits is too difficult; that you are too "weak" to change. Your old self, often so comfortable living with bad habits, is trying to hold on. Breaking your old patterns may require meditation and prayer.

Visualize regularly the rewards for following through and the costs of not following through on breaking the bad habits and especially the value to your future of building new better habits.

Get support from others, especially other people who want to make changes in their lives and read about people who have been successful in breaking bad habits. Affirm that, no matter what, you will not backslide into your old bad habit patterns.

Now, you are armed with a 5-step process for breaking any bad habit or other condition that requires changing. If you have an addiction to something such as alcohol, these steps alone may not be enough. You may require additional professional help or a support group, but for most cases, this 5-step process will do the trick!

52201668R00101

Made in the USA
Lexington, KY
10 September 2019